LESSONS FROM ROMANS 8

FROM HERE TO *Eternity*

Assurance in the face of sin and suffering

RAY GALEA

LESSONS FROM ROMANS 8

FROM HERE TO Eternity

Assurance in the face
of sin and suffering

RAY GALEA

SYDNEY · YOUNGSTOWN

From Here to Eternity
© Ray Galea 2017

All rights reserved. Except as may be permitted by the Copyright Act, no part of this publication may be reproduced in any form or by any means without prior permission from the publisher. Please direct all copyright enquiries and permission requests to the publisher.

Matthias Media
(St Matthias Press Ltd ACN 067 558 365)
Email: info@matthiasmedia.com.au
Internet: www.matthiasmedia.com.au
Please visit our website for current postal and telephone contact information.

Matthias Media (USA)
Email: sales@matthiasmedia.com
Internet: www.matthiasmedia.com
Please visit our website for current postal and telephone contact information.

Scripture taken from the Holy Bible, NEW INTERNATIONAL VERSION®, NIV®. Copyright © 1973, 1978, 1984, 2011 by Biblica, Inc. All rights reserved worldwide. Used by permission.

ISBN 978 1 925424 10 2

Cover design and typesetting by Lankshear Design.

This book is dedicated to my longest-standing
Christian friends,
Phil and Anne Gilchrist and Kimberly and
Stephen Sawyer,
whose fellowship and friendship I count as one
of God's precious gifts to me.

Contents

Foreword	9
Introduction	13

Part I: The Spirit and the sinful nature (Romans 8:1-17) — 21

1. What the law could not do	23
2. Weakened by the flesh	39
3. No condemnation for those in Christ	49
4. The power of the Spirit to transform	63
5. The presence of the Spirit	79
6. The Spirit of sonship	95

Part II: Living with suffering (Romans 8:17-39) — 111

7. Now you cry "Why?", but then…	117
8. Groaning for glory	125
9. We groan, and the Spirit groans for us	135
10. God is in the thick of it	147
11. Thinking really big picture	163
12. What then shall we say in response?	181
Conclusion	199
Acknowledgements	203

Appendices 205
A. Romans 8 207
B. Setting the scene: Romans 1-7 211
C. On predestination 219
D. Romans 8 in 44 key ideas 225
E. On the death of a grandson (by Phillip Jensen) 231

Foreword

You're about to encounter the combination of Ray Galea and Romans 8. And I couldn't be happier for you, because it's a combination that changed my life.

In the mid-1990s, a group of friends—one guy in particular—patiently and persistently invited me to return to the church where I had grown up. I'd abandoned the church and run away from God as a teenager, but my friend didn't give up on me. Nor did God.

In September 1997, I finally relented and came back to church for the first time in about five years. Over the next few months, God used the faithful weekly preaching from the Bible—along with the godly example of church members plus several conversations with friends (praise God for late-night trips to McDonald's)—to soften my heart to the truth. But he used Romans 8 and Ray Galea to bring it all together and close the deal.

In January 1998, a group of young adults from my church went away to a Bible teaching convention a couple of hours outside Sydney. Though I was ready to commit to a weekend away, I really didn't know what I was getting myself in for. But that weekend ended up being a turning point in my life.

Ray Galea was a speaker at that conference, and his four

talks came from a single chapter of the Bible: Romans 8. I had no idea who Ray was, and I had only the barest inkling of the treasures that awaited me in Romans. In fact, when I first saw the weekend's program, I vaguely remember thinking, "Four talks from just one chapter of the Bible—really?!?"

Little did I know.

By the end of that weekend, everything had changed. As I listened to Ray preach from Romans 8, I saw reality as I had never seen it before. I caught a glimpse of God's sweeping plans for the universe and for history, and how I fitted into those plans. I heard about the power and the presence of the Holy Spirit in the lives of God's people, and learned that life now will be about continuing to struggle with sin, continuing to deal with suffering as we long for the glory that awaits us. I heard that nothing in all creation could derail what God is doing or separate me from his love. I understood—in my heart and my soul, not just in my head—that Jesus Christ stands at the centre of it all, and that it was his death and resurrection that enabled me to be reconciled to God, to escape the condemnation that I deserve. I finally knew that I needed to stop running from God, and bow the knee to Jesus. So I did.

I ended that weekend a changed man, having put my trust in Jesus as my Saviour for the first time, resolving to follow Jesus as Lord from then on. But that was just the beginning.

About 18 months later, I attended another conference where Ray was speaking. I thought he might be encouraged to hear my story, so I approached him after his talk and told him about how I'd become a Christian as I listened to him preach from Romans 8. As I shared my story, Ray listened, smiled gently, then said just one thing to me: "Spend the rest of your life praising God for it!"

As I've tried to follow Ray's simple, pitch-perfect advice, it turns out that the truths I heard on that fateful weekend in 1998 are the same truths that have sustained me through the ups-and-downs of the last two decades. And there are very few places in Scripture that illuminate those truths more powerfully and clearly than Romans 8. Time and time again, I've returned to the place where it all began—this majestic and glorious chapter, quite possibly the greatest chapter in all of Scripture. Every time I read it, new treasures emerge. I sometimes feel as though I've barely scratched the surface.

All of that explains why I love this book, and why I'm thrilled that you're reading it.

They say the Grand Canyon is one of those rare natural wonders that never disappoints, no matter how high your expectations or how many times you've already seen it. Romans 8 is like that. No matter how many times you've read these words, no matter what riches you might expect or how long and hard you've pondered these realities, this is one chapter that will never disappoint. It will continue to yield new treasures, if you're willing to dig deep. The effort we put into Romans 8 will be repaid to us a hundredfold.

In an age where more and more of us possess the attention span of an amnesiac goldfish, flitting from one distraction to the next at breakneck speed, *From Here to Eternity* is a book to help you stop and linger in a place that deserves our undivided, sustained attention. And just like a good tour guide helps you to make the most of a spectacular natural wonder, so Ray's insights, practical wisdom, and passion for the glory of God serve as the ideal guide to the life-changing and faith-sustaining truths of this most wondrous chapter.

This book is a treasure for living the Christian life, no

matter how long you've been walking with Jesus. May your life be changed as mine was, and is, by Romans 8.

Geoff Robson

Introduction

About a quarter before nine, while he was describing the change which God works in the heart through faith in Christ, I felt my heart strangely warmed. I felt I did trust Christ, Christ alone, for salvation; and an assurance was given me that He had taken away my sins, even mine, and saved me from the law of sin and death.[1]

—John Wesley, referring to his experience on Aldersgate Street

Josephine was the Lebanese mother of one of the young men at my church. As her husband's coffin was being lowered into the ground, she kept crying out a single phrase in Arabic. I asked an Arabic-speaking friend what she was saying. He told me she was saying, "I'm so jealous, I'm so jealous, I'm so jealous".

Josephine was so sure that God would keep his promises,

---

1 Percy Livingstone Parker (ed.), *The Heart of John Wesley's Journal*, Hendrickson, Peabody, 2008, p. 66. Wesley describes going "very unwillingly" to a society that met on Aldersgate Street, where he heard a reading from Martin Luther's preface to the epistle to the Romans.

and so certain that her husband was with Christ, that she was left with a proper jealousy, craving to be where he was. This was more than just a grieving widow wishing her own life would end, and it was anything but wishful thinking. It was a sure and certain hope.

It is far too common to find born-again Christians who see eternity with God as uncertain. Perhaps this is your burden. You walk the Christian life as if it were an emotional roller coaster where every sin puts you out of God's love, and every good work pulls you back in. You're only as confident as your last good deed. You may even have learnt to talk the talk when it comes to assurance—others might hear you utter words of confidence and assume you're like those Welsh Christians in the early 20th-century revivals who were known as 'The Assured Ones'—but deep down you are filled with haunting doubts that steal your joy and cripple your service. Maybe you feel like the girl plucking the petals from a daisy, rehearsing the same words to herself over and over: "He loves me, he loves me not; he loves me, he loves me not."

But did you know that it's important to God not only that he saves you through his Son, the Lord Jesus, but also **that you know you are saved**? God wants you to *know* that "there is now no condemnation for those who are in Christ Jesus" (Rom 8:1).

Assurance is one of the most precious and important gifts that any Christian can possess. Martyn Lloyd-Jones, often regarded as one of the great preachers of the 20th century, highlights what is at stake when assurance is missing:

We should all be concerned about our assurance of salvation, because if we lack assurance we lack joy, and if we lack joy our life is probably of a poor quality. 'The joy of the Lord is your strength' (Nehemiah 8:10).[2]

The reality is, however, that we all live with a degree of doubt. Unlike 'disbelief', which belongs to the non-Christian, doubts find their place in the corners of all our hearts to some extent.

I invited members of my church to share their doubts. Some are listed below, and they are typical of the range of issues that afflict Christians:

- I'm 30, I grew up in a Christian home, and I often wonder: is this my faith, or my parents' faith?
- I read that there is no condemnation for those in Christ, but I feel rejected by God.
- I live with constant pain, and I find it hard to experience God's saving love.
- I live with the constant fear of deceiving myself that I am really a child of God.
- How many times will God forgive my repeated sin? I fear there must be a limit!
- I think to myself, "Unless my faith is perfect (minus any doubt), then it can't be true faith".
- If my works are evidence for my faith then how many works are required, and of what type?
- I fear that I may have put my faith in my works and not in Jesus.

---

2 D Martyn Lloyd-Jones, *Romans*, vol. 7, *The Sons of God: Exposition of Chapter 8:5-17*, Banner of Truth, Edinburgh, 1974, p. 16.

- When I compare myself with other Christians, I don't have their joy or respond to trials with the same maturity.
- Is Jesus really God, or are the Jehovah's Witnesses right?
- Is the Bible really God's word, given how the New Testament canon was formed?

And the list goes on and on…

Based on these reflections, there are at least three categories of doubts that Christians experience:

- Some are unsure that the Bible's teaching is true (e.g. the Bible may say it, but did Jesus really rise from the dead?).
- Some doubt whether they have a correct understanding of the Bible's teaching (e.g. does the Bible really say that Jesus is God?).
- Still others know that Christianity is true, but they remain unsure whether they are included in God's saving purposes (e.g. am I really forgiven? Has God chosen me?).

Romans 8 will especially speak to a number of doubts within the second and third categories.

Does it matter if we don't experience assurance? It's worth stating that the experience of assurance of salvation is not the same as the salvation itself. Rather, assurance is a blessing that flows out from the gospel of our Lord Jesus. For example, you can be a genuine Christian and be poorly taught, or you may battle with mental health issues. There are many reasons you may be a Christian and yet not experience much certainty around your status in Christ. However, this is not God's intention for his people.

Romans 8 is the most extraordinary chapter in the Bible, in part because it wants to drown us in a sea of certainty. The apostle Paul opens the chapter with a stunning truth: "there is now *no condemnation* for those who are in Christ Jesus" (v. 1). None! Then as the chapter concludes, Paul declares that *nothing in all creation* "will be able to separate us from the love of God that is in Christ Jesus our Lord" (v. 39).

Many years ago, while our family was driving along a coastal road, my then four-year-old son James piped up from the back seat: "Dad, why don't we just drive over the cliff? That way we can die and go straight to heaven." While I had to remind him that only God has the right to say when we come home, there was a confident, childlike trust that saw death in Christ as a gateway into the arms of God himself. My son was experiencing the assurance that he was entitled to as a child of God. Even at that age, he knew that being with God in heaven would be far better than life in this broken world. In essence, he simply wanted to reduce the gap between now and then.

But like it or not, life is lived in the here-and-now. We live from here to eternity.[3] Our life in Christ is lived in this age—where we are justified, and where we eagerly await the glory that lies ahead. But between those two certainties, we are confronted with two realities in this age: sin and suffering.

Our experience of sin and suffering can undermine our

---

3 I first came across the expression 'from here to eternity' as the title of the classic 1953 film. The title was originally drawn from Rudyard Kipling's 1892 poem *Gentlemen-Rankers*, about British soldiers who had lost their way and were "Damned from here to Eternity". How different that is from the theme of Romans 8, which is all about us being saved from here to eternity. No matter how badly we may have lost our way, God can save us!

hope and our assurance. In 1654, the Puritan Thomas Brooks wrote:

> Most Christians live between fears and hopes, and hang, as it were, between heaven and hell. Sometimes they hope that their state is good, at other times they fear that their state is bad: now they hope that all is well, and that it shall go well with them forever; [then] they fear that they shall perish by the hand of such a corruption, or by the prevalence of such or such a temptation… They are like a ship in a storm, tossed here and there.[4]

As we will see in Romans 8, the apostle Paul seeks to reassure us of the *certainty* of our hope in the face of pain and recurring sin.

In a sense this has never been more important, given that life expectancy in the Western world has improved dramatically. In Australia, "boys and girls born in 2013-2015 can expect to live around 33 and 34 years longer respectively [than those born just over a century earlier]".[5] There is now an extra 30+ years on the table for many of us (God willing). A longer life brings more opportunities to glorify God, but it also brings more challenges to overcome. And that means an extra 30+ years of remaining content, staying faithful to your spouse, managing your temper, enduring pain, staying passionate for Christ, and generally being other-person

---

4 Thomas Brooks, *Heaven on Earth: A Treatise on Christian Assurance*, Banner of Truth, London, 1961 (originally published 1654), p. 11.
5 Australian Institute of Health and Welfare, 'Life expectancy', AIHW, Canberra, 2016 (viewed 1 June 2017): www.aihw.gov.au/deaths/life-expectancy.

centred. It means 30+ years of opportunity for some kind of sin or some kind of suffering—those two constant companions, those two never-ending hurdles in our lives in this age—to derail our walk with Jesus.

If life is lived from here to eternity, it is a long 'here'.

This is where Romans 8 comes in.

In the first section of this book, we will look at how God works to overcome not just the *penalty* of sin, but also the controlling *power* of sin. God will not allow our sinful weakness to rob us of our place in glory. In short, God's gifts of his Son and the indwelling presence of his Spirit mean that obedience is not only possible; it is assumed and expected. By emphasizing this great reality, Paul puts to rest any accusation that the good news concerning Jesus is a licence to sin. Rather, God *will* change us; he will do what the law on its own could never do. Yet as we live out our new life in Christ, each Christian still faces an ongoing battle with sin and the 'sinful nature'. But this battle takes place from 'within the family', with God as our Father being for us, not against us.

At the end of each chapter in part I, as an example of how we might engage in this struggle with sin, I will reflect on my personal struggle with anger and how the truths taught in Romans 8 have helped me in my lifelong battle with my temper.

In the second section of the book, we will shift our focus to the topic of suffering. We'll see that the hardships of this life are actually part of God's plan in this fallen creation, not a denial of his love. Suffering is a necessary element in allowing us to reach maturity in Christ. At the end of each chapter in part II, I have invited a number of people who have battled and are battling with suffering to tell their stories and to reflect on how they have been sustained by the truths revealed in Romans 8.

If you'd appreciate some help getting oriented to the whole of Romans before you jump into chapter 8, I've included a summary of Romans 1-7 at the end of this book (see appendix B). You can also find the full text of Romans 8 printed in appendix A; I recommend reading it in one go before we start our step-by-step journey through the chapter.

In Romans 8, Paul doesn't pretend that life is a bed of roses. He maintains a healthy realism about the Christian life, and makes clear that God expects his people to groan in a broken world with a quota of pain. An ongoing battle with sin is also expected. There is no promise of an unachievable perfectionism this side of glory, no promise of heaven on earth. I am not forced to pretend that my life is one endless victory after another. But neither am I left with a pessimistic Christianity where I am always filled with doubt, always defeated by sin, never making progress. Throughout Romans 8, Paul emphatically and repeatedly affirms that neither sin nor suffering will drive a wedge between the love of Christ and us. Too often, Christians misread recurring sin and ongoing suffering, and in so doing they allow their walk with Jesus to be hijacked.

Throughout the journey of this life, the God and Father of our Lord Jesus Christ not only wants to save his people; he wants us to **know** that we are saved. May you come to know this, and so much more, as you study Romans 8.

Part I

THE SPIRIT AND THE SINFUL NATURE

ROMANS 8:1-17

1
What the law could not do
Romans 8:3a

For what the law was powerless to do because it was weakened by the flesh, God did… (Rom 8:3a)

Humans are instinctively religious. As we battle with our failure to be what we want to be, and what God wants us to be, our default position is to go back to some kind of law to keep us on track. We search for lists of dos and don'ts, and we hope that keeping enough rules and observing enough laws might atone for our failings.

Christianity is not this kind of 'religion', and yet the law of God plays a central role in the Bible's unfolding storyline. Therefore, we need to grasp the purpose of the law of God: what it is intended to do and, importantly, not do. In this chapter, we explore the positive yet powerless role of the law of God to motivate obedience on its own. It is critical that we 'get' the purpose of the law, which includes understanding its limitations.

Our inability to keep the law

Yahoo! News once asked adults who admit that they text (or email or use apps like 'Words with Friends') while driving to share brief personal anecdotes of a recent experience. Michael Strauss told his story:

> Whenever I see people texting while driving, I get furious. When any of my friends text while driving, I call them out on it. Naturally, I am a hypocrite.
>
> Despite my avowed hatred for texting while driving, I found myself doing it in September last year. A friend had called me during work with very important news. Because I was at work, I had to put her off, but I promised to contact her as soon as I got off work. She told me she might not be able to answer the phone at that time, but could receive texts.
>
> My ethics were simply thrown out the window. As soon as I got into the car, I started texting her to let her know I was free if she wanted to talk. I kept my text short and tried to do it only while stopped at a traffic light, but that wasn't entirely possible. I don't know the laws in Pennsylvania for certain, but I think it was illegal and I felt guilty the entire time.[6]

Like Michael, we all try to live by some kind of law. We each carry our own moral code. Life is filled with a quota of 'oughts' and 'shoulds' that drive our decisions or wound

---

6 'Guilt, shame and stubbornness: What adults feel while texting and driving', *Yahoo! News*, 28 March 2013 (viewed 4 September 2013): www.news.yahoo.com/guilt-shame-stubbornness-adults-feel-while-texting-driving-214000006.html.

our conscience. Some of these 'oughts' are shared within our community, and some are peculiar to us as individuals. If you struggle with Obsessive Compulsive Disorder, you impose more 'oughts' on yourself than most people.

Our codes affect us in strange ways. For example, we may feel proud when we keep our own moral code by putting our rubbish in the bin at McDonald's. And we might look down on those who leave their trash sitting there on the table. Or we might be petrified that others could find out that we have failed to live up to our own principles by texting in the car. You may have experienced the nightmare of an ex-lover uploading those taboo private photos to Facebook, or the shame and embarrassment of having your worst moments laid bare.

Many may be 'losing their religion', as the R.E.M. song says, but they have not lost a personal sense of right and wrong. These 'shoulds' and 'oughts' that we live by can feel as real and authoritative as the very words of God given at Mount Sinai. More often than not, we are born into a culture with a strong current of unquestioned beliefs that causes many of us to adopt certain values with little reflection—until they get in the way of what we want.

But whether we are talking of a personal moral code, the law given at Mount Sinai to the Jews, or the law of Christ for the New Covenant believer (see 1 Cor 9:20-21), we all eventually discover that we fall short of whatever standard we have chosen for ourselves.

Which of the following age-old solutions to this problem do you identify with?

- You let your moral successes 'buy off' or atone for your failures.

- You highlight to others and yourself those 'oughts' in which you appear to do well.
- You suppress your guilt by either pain or pleasure.
- You live a life of endless distractions to keep from introspection.
- You modify your personal moral code to suit your present lifestyle choices.
- You reduce your moral code to fewer and fewer 'oughts' as you get older, if for no other reason than life is short and feeling guilty is a drag.
- You focus on the failings of others, and compare yourself favourably.

So the Ten Commandments become the Ten Suggestions, which are then further reduced to two or three mild convictions, until finally all you're left with is a vague principle that says, "Be nice!" And this is not just a religious problem. Atheists have the same battle, for they too have a moral code that they also break at times, violating their own conscience.

Everyone experiences guilt, whether it is legitimate or not, and each person has their own way of coping with it. Some years ago, while staying overnight at a friend's home, I spilt coffee on the brand new and very stylish Norwegian raw timber bedside table. I knew I was in serious trouble. My first attempt to deal with my guilt was to not tell my friend, but to clean the stain myself. I went on YouTube to research different methods of coffee-stain removal. But no matter what I did, I couldn't get rid of it. My next strategy was to use the base of the lamp stand to cover up the stain, hoping my friend wouldn't see it. The third step was to tell myself it wasn't all that bad and that the stain added character to the table, all while trying to manage the guilt myself and avoid the possible anger of my host.

On a grander scale, the rise of psychotherapy may in part be the fruit of people's search for a resolution of their guilt. GK Chesterton once said that psychoanalysis is confession without absolution.[7] Yet sometimes counsellors take that next step by offering strategies to cleanse consciences and absolve guilt. They do so with good intent, wanting to comfort their clients with words such as, "Given the pressure you were under, it's fully understandable that you did what you did".

Amid all the possible approaches to guilt, Christianity has, to my mind, the most profound and radical reflection on the role of the law and the reality of guilt. Unlike our personal moral codes, the Bible records God giving his objective law— in history, on public record—at Mount Sinai (Exodus 20). He did that only after he had graciously saved his people from their enslavement in Egypt (Deuteronomy 5). That law defined how the God of Abraham was to be loved and worshipped, and how his people were to relate to each other and the world.

However, like every form of moral code, it could not inspire obedience. In fact, it proved to be impotent: "For what the law was *powerless* to do because it was weakened by the flesh, God did…" (Rom 8:3).

Romans 8:1-4 closes out a discussion on the ineffectiveness of the law of God to produce change and give life (7:10). That discussion began back in Romans 7. So before looking

---

7   See Ralph A Connell, 'The Church and Psychiatry', *America*, 30 July 2001 (viewed 13 April 2017): www.americamagazine.org/issue/325/article/church-and-psychiatry.

at the opening verses of chapter 8 in detail, let's take a step back to the previous chapter so we can understand the place of the law.

The purpose of the law

In Romans 7, Paul reflects on the purpose of the law of God and describes how and why the law cannot overcome the controlling power of sin in our lives. On its own, the law leaves us as prisoners of sin. This is captured in the desperate cry at the end of Romans 7: "What a wretched man I am! Who will rescue me from this body that is subject to death?" (v. 24).

By 'the law of God', the apostle means the 613 commandments found in the Old Testament, summarized in the Ten Commandments, and summarized further in the call of Jesus to love God with all of your being and to love your neighbour as yourself (Matt 22:37-38; Mark 12:30-31).

In Romans 7, the law of God works like a double agent. In the movie *Salt*, it's unclear for most of the film whether the main character, played by Angelina Jolie, is an American spy or a Russian double agent. Likewise, it sometimes appears unclear whether the law of God is an agent of sin or a gift from God.

On the one hand, the law clearly comes from God. It is viewed as "holy, righteous and good" (7:12), and is clearly necessary to teach us exactly what qualifies as sin: "What shall we say, then? Is the law sinful? Certainly not! Nevertheless, I would not have known what sin was had it not been for the law" (7:7). God's law reveals God's character by drawing a line in the sand to tell us what pleases him and what grieves him.

On the other hand, there is a sense in which the law does more harm than good. John Calvin rightly notes that while the law teaches righteousness, it cannot confer it.[8] The problem is clearly not with the law. In every relationship, we need boundary markers to define how we should relate to each other. The problem, as Romans 7 tells us, is that the law of God is exploited by the power of sin for its own sinful purposes.[9] Listen to Paul's description of this dynamic—one that every Christian knows all too well:[10] "But sin, seizing the opportunity afforded by the commandment, produced in me every kind of coveting" (7:8).

On its own, the law of God is depicted as being a bit like a nagging spouse, a demanding boss, a graceless pastor, a controlling parent who micromanages your life with a series of 'do this, don't do that' directives. But the most frustrating thing about a nagger is that they are often right. I *should* pick up my clothes. I *should* lose weight. I *should* visit my mother-in-law more often. I *should* pray more regularly. I *should* speak up for those who can't speak up for themselves. But even if a nagger is right, we all know nagging is ineffective. In fact, it brings out the rebel in us. This is one of the core conclusions

---

8   John Calvin, *Commentaries on the Epistle of Paul the Apostle to the Romans*, chapter VIII, ed. and trans. John Owen, Bibliolife, Charleston, 2009 [1849], p. 276.

9   Sin here is not individual acts of rebellion, but is personified as a force or power that operates within the heart of every human. This is seen, for example, in 7:8, where 'sin' is said to produce 'coveting', even though covetousness is clearly a form of sin.

10   For more on whether Paul refers to the Christian or the non-Christian throughout chapter 7, see appendix B. I take the view that Paul speaks from the Christian's perspective.

of Romans 7. The law doesn't motivate; rather than reducing sin, it inflames it. The dos and don'ts of the law act like a catalyst for sin when they reach the ears of sinful human beings.

John Piper helpfully illustrates the misuse of the law by sin:

> Picture the Law as a surgeon's scalpel. It is meant for life and healing. And here comes sin and takes the scalpel of God's commandments and slashes people's throats with it… The commandment—holy, just, good—was to be life to me, and it became death for me, because sin took the scalpel out of the surgeon's hand and with it slashed my throat and killed me (verse 10). That is not what a scalpel is for.[11]

The law increases sin

From the beginning, God knew that when he gave the Ten Commandments in a fallen world, sin would increase, not decrease. That is exactly what happened, and that is why Paul can say, "the law brings wrath" (4:15) and "the law was brought in so that the trespass might increase" (5:20a).

The law does to sin what fertilizer does to my lawn: it makes it grow! Or to put it another way, the effect of the law on sin is not unlike the effect of shaking a can of Coke. As Paul says elsewhere, "the power of sin is the law" (1 Cor 15:56). The law, manipulated by sin, adds fuel to the fire of our rebellion, despite our best intentions.

---

11   John Piper, 'The deadly team of sin and law', *Desiring God*, 6 May 2001 (viewed 13 April 2017): www.desiringgod.org/resource-library/sermons/the-deadly-team-of-sin-and-law.

Some time ago, I did what I call 'the Romans 7 test'. My wife, Sandy, was coming into the house with bags in hand after some serious shopping. I said to her, "Sandy, whatever you do, don't read page eight of *The Star*" (the local newspaper that was lying on the kitchen table). Sure enough, without any hesitation, she went straight to page eight and asked, "What don't you want me to look at?" You know the experience. You see a sign that clearly reads, "Wet paint: Do not touch!" and before you know it you are wiping the paint off your hands.

There is a classic example of this dynamic at the end of the book of Joshua. Joshua had led God's people into the Promised Land. On his deathbed, he renewed the covenant and gave final instructions to Israel. Compare the people's optimism with Joshua's pessimism:

Joshua: Now fear the Lord and serve him with all faithfulness…

The people: Far be it from us to forsake the Lord to serve other gods…

Joshua: You are not able to serve the Lord. He is a holy God; he is a jealous God…

The people: No! We will serve the Lord.

Joshua: You are witnesses against yourselves that you have chosen to serve the Lord.

The people: Yes, we are witnesses. (Josh 24:14-22)

Then we turn ahead two pages in our Bible, and we read of the tragedy of the next generation:

> Then the Israelites did evil in the eyes of the Lord and served the Baals. They forsook the Lord, the God of their ancestors, who had brought them out of Egypt. They followed and worshiped various gods of the peoples around them. They aroused the Lord's anger… (Judg 2:11-12)

The law of God has many roles in God's plan, but saving people is not one of them. Nor is it the law's job to motivate people to do the right thing.[12] That is why it's called "the law of sin and death" (Rom 8:2). The law produces more sin and leads to our death. In one sense, Israel was the test case: the Israelites were under the law, privileged with election and entrusted with the oracles and commands of God. But as the Old Testament testifies, the children of Abraham, chosen to be a light to the pagan nations, mirrored the behaviour of the nations and in fact were accused of being worse than the nations. The result, anticipated from the beginning, was both the exile (Deut 28:36, 64) and the execution of the long-awaited Messiah.

This law dynamic probably explains why reverse psychology works: sinful people tend to do the opposite of what they are told to do.

In 1982, Timothy Wilson and Daniel Lassiter conducted a study to show how reverse psychology works. It involved creating a desire for a toy that at first was not appealing. The authors of the experiment chose the one toy that was least played with by a group of children. The children were then

---

[12] Although both Old Testament believers (Ps 19:7-10) and Spirit-filled disciples can see wisdom's beautiful face in God's law (Jas 1:25).

divided into two groups. The first group was told they could play with any toy they liked. The second group was told they could play with any toy except one: the toy they had played with the least. What the researchers found was that when both groups were again allowed to play with the forbidden toy, the children in the second group played with it for three times longer.[13]

The experiment reminds us of what we all know to be true in our experience: on its own, any law incites within us the opposite response.

Left to ourselves, without the Spirit, we are prisoners of the law of sin (Rom 7:23), and as prisoners we are both powerless and condemned: "For when we were in the realm of the flesh, the sinful passions aroused by the law were at work in us, so that we bore fruit for death" (7:5). Hence Paul's exasperated cry, "What a wretched man I am! Who will rescue me from this body that is subject to death?" (7:24).

We need to be set free.

Notice how the Bible's view of the law differs from most, if not all, religions. Religion promises that obedience to its holy and spiritual laws, principles, or wise insights is achievable with human effort, or with sincerity, or with communal encouragement, or through some meditative technique. If only you want it enough, or believe enough, or know enough, you can obey. The power lies within you. In essence, religion abandons people to their own resources, and to a standard that their human will can't keep.

---

13 Magda Kay, 'How to use reverse psychology to make others do what you want', *Psychology for Marketers*, no date (viewed 13 April 2017): www.psychologyformarketers.com/how-to-use-reverse-psychology.

That is why religion, with all its dos and don'ts, is a dead end and will always be a dead end. It generates either pride for those who appear to obey, or a sense of fear or failure for those who know they don't live up to the standards.

And yet, if God is personal and he has expressed his will—including a prominent place for the law—then having no law can't be a solution. But as we will see in the next chapter, the problem is not the law of God. The problem is me.

My battle with anger

It happened again!

The youth were celebrating their last meeting of the year with a formal dinner. The mood was positive, and rightly so. Our previous youth pastor had left with our blessing to plant a church, taking the youth leadership team with him. And now the new youth pastor and his wonderful team had had an extraordinary and fruitful year.

As I went around congratulating the team, I unwittingly expressed my exasperation with the state of the chairs to our youth pastor, doing so in front of the other youth leaders. I was so self-absorbed that I didn't even notice the damage I did to the youth leadership team until the next morning.

I'm tired of being the grumpy old pastor.

My congregation knows that my anger has been a constant area of weakness in my character. And even if most never see it, my family and staff have certainly experienced me at my worst.

Any attempt to blame the pressure of ministry, a father

with a short fuse, or my ethnic baggage (Maltese are known for being angry) is a dead end. They are neither explanations nor excuses. The law of God is clear: any ungodly display of anger is sin. It is possible to be angry and not sin (Eph 4:26), but this has not been my experience. It is all the more serious given that the pastor-elder is to be marked by gentleness (e.g. 1 Tim 6:11; Titus 1:7). The first word used to describe love in 1 Corinthians 13 is 'patient', and without this kind of love we are nothing—a waste of space!

I do believe in 'righteous anger'; both God and Jesus demonstrate it repeatedly throughout the Scriptures. It's also true to say that sometimes we are simply not angry enough— for example, when it comes to sexual abuse in the church, or the fate of the unborn. So often human anger does spring from a righteous concern. But it almost always ends up corrupted by a harsh comment, a passive sulk, or a sarcastic jibe that exposes the problem of the heart.

I may on occasion take comfort in the fact that I am not a violent man, but that is only because I am often unaware of the damage done by my demanding words, my harsh tone, or my vengeful silence—all of which spring from a heart that, according to Jesus, is effectively guilty of the sin of murder (Matt 5:21-22). And the book of James reminds me that my sinful display of anger never produces the righteousness that God requires (Jas 1:20).

Without exception, I have always regretted pouring forth or leaking out my wrath. I can't think of one time when I said to myself after an overreaction, "I'm so glad I got that off my chest". The unrighteous display of anger has a 100% failure rate. It's my gentleness that needs to be evident to all, not my temper.

In all of this, knowing the role of the law is very helpful. Its prime task is to reflect God's righteous character and to define how we ought to live. The wisdom of the law teaches me that anger resides in the heart of the fool (Eccl 7:9). Jesus declared that the heart that leads to murder and the heart that produces anger spring from the same well.

When you're on the receiving end of anger it's clear that God's law is good, as it protects people from unrighteous displays of anger. As RC Sproul writes, "The law allows for a limited measure of justice on this earth, until the last judgment is realized".[14] God speaks up for us when we are on the receiving end of rage, cynicism, verbal abuse and physical violence. God also entrusts to governments and other authorities the right to restrain sin, including the violent expression of anger, through their laws (Rom 13:3-4). Even Truman Capote acknowledged the value of the law when he said, "The problem with living outside the law is that you no longer have its protection".

When you're the cause of that anger, however, the rebuke of God's law is hard to hear. Seeing through God's eyes the seriousness of anger and the damage done to his image-bearers is critical. God has drawn the line in the sand. I have learnt to say to myself, "My anger is always worse than the thing I am angry about".

On occasion, my mother warned me of the dangerous consequences of my temper. She even voiced her fear that I would commit a crime of passion, resulting in imprisonment. But that only made me angrier. I certainly did not see

---

14   RC Sproul, *Essential Truths of the Christian Faith*, Tyndale, Carol Stream, 1998, p. 267.

the 'evil face' of my anger for the first 20 years of my life, when I did not know Christ or the power of his Spirit. The law, expressed through my mother's wise instruction, fell on deaf ears until I was born again of God's Spirit.

Even now, as a believer, the law of God on its own still won't change my struggle with anger. I hate my anger, and I hate what it does to my loved ones—and so does God. I see the damage that's been done when I ask others how they feel when I speak with an angry tone. When asked for feedback about my anger, one of my staff said, "I'm not sure which Ray I am going to get" (happy Ray or grumpy Ray).

Allowing God's law to name the seriousness of the sin of anger is the first important step. Seeing the wisdom of God in his law is equally important. I can see that God's way is indeed the best way. And yet, on its own, this law leaves me powerless and overwhelmed in guilt. I cannot change if all I have is "In your anger do not sin" (Eph 4:26).

I must keep reading.

2
Weakened by the flesh
Romans 8:3a

For what the law was powerless to do because it was **weakened by the flesh**, God did… (Rom 8:3a)

CS Lewis wrote, "No man knows how bad he is till he has tried very hard to be good".[15]

If the law of God is neither the solution nor the core problem, as we saw in the previous chapter, then who or what is the cause of my sin? While it would be so natural to point the finger at someone or something else and say, "You made me do it", the diagnosis according to Jesus and the apostle Paul is both internal and profound. Without wanting to deny the role of bad parenting, genetic dispositions, dysfunctional relationships, the schemes of the devil, and the patterns of the world, we are forced to own full responsibility for each and every one of our sins. In the words of Paul, "good itself does not dwell in me, that is, in my sinful nature" (Rom 7:18).

---

15 CS Lewis, *Mere Christianity*, HarperOne, New York, 2015, p. 142.

Our sinful nature

Moment of Truth was an American reality game show that ran for two years. Like many of these reality game shows, a correct answer gets you the money—but this show came with a twist. On camera, with a live audience present and in front of family and friends, the contestants were asked a string of questions about their personal life with their answers being analysed by a lie detector.

On one occasion, a female contestant named Lauren Cleri was far enough along in the 'game' that one more true answer would net her $100,000. But if she gave a false answer, she would leave with nothing. Lauren was asked a question by a 'surprise guest': her ex-boyfriend. He asked: "If I wanted to get back together with you, would you leave your husband?"

She paused, then reluctantly admitted that she would leave her husband for this other man. "There goes that marriage", I thought to myself. But she had won $100,000, and now needed just three more true answers for another $100,000. The host asked the next question: "Since you've been married, have you ever had sexual relations with someone other than your husband?" Again Lauren paused, looked at her husband, and then finally conceded, "Yes". Now I'm thinking to myself, "She is really committed to getting as much money as possible, whatever the cost".

Then came the next question—one step closer to more money with a true answer, or nothing but a whole lot of embarrassment and pain with a false answer. After the previous bombshells, this question seemed simple: **"Do you think you're a good person?"**

Given what she had done, this was a no-brainer. With so

much riding on the question and given that she was already prepared to ruin her marriage for the money, it seemed clear that she would tell the truth and say, "No!"

But to the surprise of everybody watching she said, "Yes, I am a good person".[16]

As Lauren Cleri gave her answer, I couldn't help but think of the words of the apostle John: "If we claim we have not sinned, we make him out to be a liar and his word is not in us" (1 John 1:10). We lie to ourselves, we lie to God, and in the process we make God out to be a liar.

As surprising as her answer was, the greater surprise came when the lie detector indicated that she was lying. At some level, Lauren Cleri must have known that she wasn't good, but even after everything else she had confessed, she was unable to publicly admit it.

Was it pride that kept her from telling the truth, even to herself? Had she blindly absorbed our culture's constant bombardment that humans are inherently good? Was the truth so suppressed that what she told herself (and others) is not what she knew deep down to be true? In Romans 1, the apostle Paul speaks of God's anger being poured out against all godlessness because people "suppress the truth" concerning who God is and how he wants us to live (v. 18). Maybe this show provides a perfect example of that suppression of truth.

It is easy to stand back and somehow think that Lauren was in a class of her own. But what this show exposed was the nature not just of one woman, but of every human: a sinful

---

16 Jeane MacIntosh, 'Wife: I did it for the TV money', *New York Post*, 27 February 2008 (viewed 13 April 2017): www.nypost.com/2008/02/27/wife-i-did-it-for-the-tv-money.

nature that is deeply flawed and rendered weak, and which, left to itself, is unable to be affected by the law of God.

The controlling power of the flesh

Let's continue to explore the idea in Romans 8:3 that the law was powerless "because it was *weakened by the flesh*".

In the previous chapter, we saw that while the law is a good gift from God, sin took advantage of the law and used it to cause an increase in rebellion. One of the purposes of Romans 7 is to provide a defence, an 'apologetic', for the law of God. The law may have its limits, but it was never the problem. It was unable, however, to produce the righteous life that God requires because it was weakened, made impotent, by the very nature of fallen humanity. The core problem is the controlling influence of the 'flesh'—what some Bible translations call the 'sinful nature'.

The 'flesh' is not the stuff that love handles are made from. Nor does the flesh only speak of our frail humanity. It refers to a mindset shaped by this world, and of a nature shared with every descendent of Adam: "For just as through the disobedience of the one man the many were made sinners…" (5:19). We sin by choice, but we also sin by nature—a nature that is born bent: "All of us also lived among them at one time, gratifying the cravings of our flesh and following its desires and thoughts. Like the rest, we were by nature deserving of wrath" (Eph 2:3). Our default position is to transgress, and all the goodwill messages in the world are not going to change that reality. Our nature is self-serving and powerless to change itself.

In an ironic twist, there is much biblical truth in hip-hop artist Macklemore's song 'Same Love': "And I can't change, even if I tried, even if I wanted to, my love".[17] Although he's rapping about the natural orientation of being gay and in support of same-sex marriage, he has stumbled onto a profound, biblical idea: the powerlessness of the flesh. In the words of Bob Dylan, "Because he [Adam] sinned I got no choice, it run in my vein".[18] Martin Luther captured it in a typically memorable phrase when he described the flesh as being "deeply curved in upon itself".[19]

The well-known fable of the scorpion and the frog illustrates this point. A scorpion wants to get to the other side of a lake. He asks a frog sitting nearby if he will carry him on his back for safe passage. Understandably the frog refuses, saying, "If I let you get on my back, you will sting me and I will die". The scorpion insists, "No I won't. I promise. Think about it: if I sting you as you carry me across the lake, you will die and I will drown. It's not to my advantage to kill you." The frog thinks about it for a moment and says, "I guess that makes sense. Climb aboard." And so off they go, with the scorpion hanging on to the frog's back.

When the frog is halfway across the lake, he feels an almighty bite on his neck. He turns to the scorpion in a state of bemused shock and cries out, "Why did you do that?" With an apologetic and resigned tone, the scorpion answers, "I couldn't help myself. *It's in my nature.*"

---

17   Macklemore and Ryan Lewis, 'Same Love' feat. Mary Lambert, 2012.
18   Bob Dylan, 'Pressing On', 1980.
19   Martin Luther, *Lectures on Romans: Glosses and Scholia*, ed. HC Oswald, trans. WG Tillmanns and JAO Preus, 1515-1516, in *Luther's Works*, 56 vols, ed. J Pelikan and H Lehmann, vol. 25, Concordia, St Louis, 1972, pp. 291, 313, 345, 513.

The fact that at least six movies and TV episodes have used this fable indicates the universal resonance of the story.[20] There was something irresistible within the nature of the scorpion that caused him to sting the frog, even though it was a suicidal act. And there is something irresistible within human nature that causes us to sin, even if we pay a mighty price to satisfy those urges.

This is why the law on its own fails to motivate obedience. Hence the popular proverb, "If you educate a devil, you only end up with a smarter devil". This describes the core weakness of humanity. It's as self-evident as the fact that you never have to teach a child to do the wrong thing. There are no classes in school to teach us to lie, or cheat, or steal—we figure it out all by ourselves. In spite of the Western world's acceptance of humanistic philosophies of education, the evidence is in favour of the Bible's world view on human nature.

Recently, one of my children—who shall remain nameless—scraped the car she was driving against a parked car. The owner was nowhere to be found. My daughter left her details on the windscreen, offering to pay for any damages. When the owner of the car called, she was both grateful and surprised that my daughter had owned up to the accident. The woman later said to me in a phone conversation, "It has restored my faith in human nature". However, her surprised reaction really confirmed that the opposite was true. The more noise we make about a good deed, the more we betray the fact that most people would have done the opposite.

---

20 I'm thinking of an episode of *Star Trek: Voyager* and the films *Mr. Arkadin* (1955), *Skin Deep* (1989), *The Crying Game* (1992), *Natural Born Killers* (1994), and *Drive* (2011).

Left to ourselves, the human equation reads:

Law + flesh = more sin + death

Or, as Paul declares, something is at work in each person "making me a prisoner of the law of sin at work within me" (Rom 7:23). This is what theologians call 'the total inability of humanity'.[21] The doctrine of total inability does not mean that human beings are as evil as they can possibly be, or that we're all just as bad as one another. What it does mean, as theologian Loraine Boettner explains, is that all humanity "possesses a fixed bias of the will against God, and instinctively and willingly turns to evil".[22] Our depravity and our inability to do what's right may express itself in various ways and to a greater or a lesser extent, but we're all rebels at heart. Somebody once asked philosopher Dallas Willard if he believed in total depravity. He responded immediately: "I believe that every human being is sufficiently depraved that when we get to heaven, no-one will be able to say, 'I merited this.'"[23]

So, what of free will? In one sense, we are 'free': our wills are not constrained by any external force. But there's a difference between 'freedom' and 'ability'. Boettner writes, "As the bird with a broken wing is 'free' to fly but not able, so the

---

21 Also called 'the total depravity (or radical depravity) of natural man', or simply 'total depravity'.
22 Loraine Boettner, *The Reformed Doctrine of Predestination*, Christian Classics Ethereal Library, Grand Rapids, 2005 (originally published 1932), chapter X, p. 44.
23 John Ortberg, 'Dallas Willard, a Man from Another "Time Zone"', *Christianity Today*, 8 May 2013 (viewed 13 April 2017): www.christianitytoday.com/ct/2013/may-web-only/man-from-another-time-zone.html.

natural man is free to come to God but not able".[24] This is why it's vital that we put our hope in God and in his saving grace, not in ourselves or in our ability to choose God. In his wonderful grace, God has not left us to ourselves. And, as we will see in the next chapter, he has not abandoned us to a nature that cannot and will not obey God's law. There is hope.

The sinful flesh and my anger

Nowhere do I see the difference between God and me more clearly than in my temper. God's anger springs from his righteous character and all-knowing (omniscient) nature, which has access to all the facts. He is the righteous judge, and his wrath is a measured, proportional, just response to sin. In contrast, my temper flows effortlessly from my sinful nature. I perceive a wrong by drawing conclusions with limited information, driven by the protection of personal needs and insecurities, and fuelled by a self-righteous and demanding spirit. And while God is slow to anger, my wrath moves with the speed of a mousetrap, slamming down on some unsuspecting fellow image-bearer. Often it flares up so quickly that I'm deceived into thinking I have no choice and I am not responsible.

Or so I thought—until one day a 'miracle' happened. I was in full flight one Saturday morning, upset about something trivial, when a knock at the door instantly changed my

---

24 Boettner, *The Reformed Doctrine*, p. 45.

demeanour. At once I was transformed into a gentle, loving pastor. Here was the evidence of what I already knew from Scripture: I am responsible, and I can change—but not on my own.

It will come as no surprise to know that the journey of transformation begins with an unqualified confession before God and others. While I was born with a sinful nature, I am responsible for the sins that flow from it. If I justify any outburst, even for a moment, then I give myself permission to lose it all over again when the next pressure point occurs. So yes, I might have been tired, and yes, they might have been cruel—but so what? "In your anger do not sin" (Eph 4:26).

I was so enslaved to the sinful nature that even seeing the sinfulness of the sin (in this case, anger) required its own miracle. I would constantly explain away the data, and trivialize the feedback on why my anger was unacceptable. Even as a Christian with the Spirit, the laboratory of marriage and parenthood managed to expose the extent of my demanding and angry desires, as well as providing the tragic opportunity to witness its devastating effects.

We each have a room at the back of our head filled with a library of rationalizations as to why we give rein to our besetting sins. I need to go to that room, plant as much C4 explosive as I can, and blow it out of existence. Only then will I begin to grow up. I have no excuse.

So how is change possible?

3

No condemnation for those in Christ
Romans 8:3-4

³ For what the law was powerless to do because it was weakened by the flesh, **God did by sending his own Son in the likeness of sinful flesh to be a sin offering.** And so he condemned sin in the flesh, ⁴ in order that the righteous requirement of the law might be fully met in us, who do not live according to the flesh but according to the Spirit. (Rom 8:3-4)

How does God solve the problem of the powerlessness of the law brought on by the power of sin and the flesh? And how is it that *now* God can declare those of us who are in Christ Jesus to be under "no condemnation" (v. 1), given that we should all be condemned by our sin?

The solution cannot come from within our nature. The last thing we need is for each of us to be 'true to our self'.

Nor is the solution found in trying a little harder to be a better person, or in changing our environment by moving to a better suburb, a finer school or a better family. These things may mean that I'm a more socially well-adjusted individual and perhaps a happier or nicer person to live with, but the flesh still makes me incapable of keeping the law of God from the heart.

Martyn Lloyd-Jones made this insightful observation:

> The terrible, tragic fallacy of the last hundred years has been to think that all man's troubles are due to his environment, and that to change the man you have nothing to do but change his environment. That is a tragic fallacy. It overlooks the fact that it was in Paradise that man fell.[25]

What then can be done?

It's helpful to see the solution to our core problem as a military-style operation that has two phases. Phase one concerns the Son, while phase two concerns the Spirit:

> For what the law was powerless to do because it was weakened by the flesh, God did by sending his own Son in the likeness of sinful flesh to be a sin offering. And so he condemned sin in the flesh, in order that the righteous requirement of the law might be fully met in us, who do not live according to the flesh but according to the Spirit. (Rom 8:3-4)

---

25   D Martyn Lloyd-Jones, *Studies in the Sermon on the Mount*, 2nd edn, IVP, Leicester, 1976, p. 110.

Phase 1: God's Son sets us free from sin

Firstly, in phase one, God sends his own Son into a world held prisoner to sin. The Son is sent behind enemy lines to set us free from our imprisonment to the tyranny of sin. It may sound like the plot line for many films, but that is in essence the correct framework of understanding.

Notice that God does not send a mere prophet to liberate his people; he does his own dirty work. Nor is the child in the manger some unlucky angel who drew the short straw in heaven; the child is God-sent, and the child is God's one and only willing Son (Phil 2:5-11).[26] We humans cry: "What a wretched man I am! Who will rescue me from this body that is subject to death?" (Rom 7:24). God says: "I will, by sending my own Son".

The Son comes fully equipped to perform the rescue operation. Take note of the delicate wording in verse 3: God sent his Son "in the likeness of sinful flesh". That is a beautifully balanced phrase that walks along the edge of two heresies: that Jesus was not human, and that he was not sinless.

An effective rescue needs to be carried out by a human. Only a human can take the sin of another human as both representative and substitute. Elsewhere we read, "it is impossible for the blood of bulls and goats to take away sins" (Heb 10:4). They only make a mess! Paul doesn't say, "God sent his own Son in the likeness of a man". Jesus was not pretending to be a human. He was and is a human.

But there is one crucial difference between Jesus' humanity and ours: 'the flesh'. Jesus shares our *human* nature, but

---

26 All this points to the fact that Jesus existed before he was born.

not our *sinful* nature. God sends his own Son *in the likeness of* sinful man, not *as* a sinful man. Only a sinless person can be in a position to die for the sins of another—otherwise, he would have to die for his own sin like the rest of us. Jesus knew no sin. He lived in between the world of temptation and transgression, but at no point did he cross the line and become a rebel like the rest of Adam's race.

When my children were young, they were amazed at the thought that Jesus never sinned. What does a sinless six-year-old look like? So I painted some pictures for them. I said to them, "This means that Jesus never had to say 'sorry' to his parents". "Really Dad?" they asked. "Yes!" I said. "There was nothing for him to apologize for. Jesus never had to be sent to his room—and if he was, it was always Mum and Dad's fault." They particularly liked this aspect of Jesus' sinlessness.

This, of course, is where the defeat of sin begins. As part of phase one, the power of sin has to be attacked from two sides before the prisoners can be released. On the positive side, Jesus needed to live a perfectly obedient life. Jesus always matched God's law with perfect obedience. Unlike Adam and unlike Israel, Jesus is the Son with whom the Father is "well pleased" (Matt 3:17, 17:5). He is the perfect covenant keeper, so that "through the obedience of the one man the many will be made righteous" (Rom 5:19b).

However, on the negative side, Jesus needed to take the punishment our sins deserve. Romans 6:23 is clear that "the wages of sin is death". Sin still needed to be condemned and God's justice needs to be satisfied, so God sends his Son to be that 'sin offering'. This is the language of sacrifice, drawn from Old Testament passages like Leviticus 4 and pointing us to the cross.[27] "God presented Christ as a sacrifice of atonement, through the shedding of his blood—to be received by faith." (Rom 3:25)

As the 'sin offering', Christ takes full responsibility for the penalty of our sin, so that we can be cleansed and forgiven. Like a lightning rod, Christ deflects God's wrath away from us and onto himself. God no longer counts our sins against us because he has counted them against his Son at the cross. The logic should read 'the wages of my sin is my death'. But now it reads, 'the wages of my sin is *his* death'. I sin; he dies. He dies; I live.

The opposite of this logic is that of Heinrich Himmler, the man who, under orders from Hitler, built the extermination camps during World War II. Himmler once said, "As an Aryan I must have the courage to take full responsibility for my sins alone".[28] Eric Metaxas writes, "He rejected as 'Jewish' the idea of putting one's sins on someone else's shoulders".[29] This is not courage; it is stupidity of cosmic proportions.

Our justification is not God playing a word game in which he arbitrarily turns the guilty into the not guilty. Our sins are only forgiven because they were already paid for at the cross. Our union with Christ through faith means our destiny is intimately bound up with Christ, so that what happens to one is counted to the other. This is not unlike a marriage,

---

27 In the Septuagint (the ancient Greek translation of the Old Testament), 44 out of 54 uses of the phrase *peri hamartias* ('concerning sin') refer to a sin offering.
28 Quoted in Eric Metaxas, *Bonhoeffer: Pastor, Martyr, Prophet, Spy*, Thomas Nelson, Nashville, 2010, p. 290.
29 Metaxas, *Bonhoeffer*, p. 290.

where the assets or debts of one partner become the assets or debts of the other.

Augustine first coined the phrase later popularized as "God hates the sin but loves the sinner".[30] But that's an oversimplification. The reality is that God saves the sinner by punishing the sin. That is why there is now "no condemnation for those who are in Christ Jesus" (Rom 8:1). The curse brought on by our natural union with Adam is now reversed for those who are in union with Christ. At the cross, sin—not the law, and not us—is condemned. Sin is punished in the body that once lay in the manger.

Jesus has assumed full responsibility for all our failures. Our Saviour picked up the bill for our life of rebellion. The result is that we are now liberated to serve, without fear, in full assurance of faith.

Tragically, not every tradition within Christianity allows its members to enjoy the God-given privilege of assurance.[31] Certainly no major world religion promises assurance—with the exception of biblical Christianity. Isma'il Ragi al Faruqi, a Muslim philosopher, helpfully contrasts Islam and biblical Christianity:

> This is why for a Christian, the very fact that he is a Christian, that is to say, the very fact that he recognizes Jesus Christ as redeemer, weighs heavily in the scales.

---

30 St Augustine's *Letter 211* (c. 424) contains the phrase *cum dilectione hominum et odio vitiorum*. A loose translation of this might be 'with love for mankind and hatred of sins'. This has become popularized as 'hate the sin and not the sinner' or 'love the sinner but hate the sin'.

31 For my own journey of coming to understand assurance, see my book *Nothing in My Hand I Bring*, Matthias Media, Sydney, 2012.

It gives him the assurance and the poise that comes from such assurance, that he is 'saved', already 'passed' deep into the second zone, and not merely lifted out of the first... Islam holds no sweet, immediate recompense to give its convert gratuitously upon conversion. On the contrary, it tells him point blank that his acceptance of Islam puts him squarely in the zero zone and lays out before him the arduous road of the Shari'ah, or Divine Law, which he has yet to tread in order to lift himself out of the zero zone by his own efforts.[32]

By contrast, what an amazing and comforting solution God has provided in sending his one and only Son. We now live with the certainty that there is no condemnation in Christ Jesus. As one Iranian man in our church who began to grasp grace for the first time said, "It's as if God is looking for an excuse to forgive us". While not technically correct, he has grasped the very heart of the God who wants to save his people, not condemn them.

And yet there is more. In Romans 8:1-4, Paul is not simply repeating his discussion on Jesus' work on the cross to justify, redeem and atone for us, as spelled out in Romans 3:21-26. In chapter 8, Paul still has in mind an accusation that was levelled at his preaching by some in Rome: "Shall we go on sinning so that grace may increase?" (6:1). To put it another way, is the death of Jesus a license to rebel?

This is where the Holy Spirit comes in.

---

32 Isma'il RA al Faruqi, *Christian Ethics: A Historical and Systematic Analysis of its Dominant Ideas*, Montreal, McGill University Press, 1967, p. 226. I am indebted to Mike Raiter and John Bales for directing me to this quote.

Phase 2: God's Spirit transforms and convicts us

In phase two of his plan, God not only sets us free from the penalty of sin but, through the work of his Spirit, he also makes us alive and sets us free from sin's controlling power. As we have already seen, Paul raised the issue of sin's controlling power in our lives back in Romans 7. Many Christians overlook the fact that God's purpose in sending his Son wasn't just to forgive his people. Romans 8:4 makes it clear that God's purpose was "in order that the righteous requirement of the law might be fully met in us". God sent his Son to be a sin offering—not just so that we would no longer *bear guilt*, but so that we might *bear fruit* (7:4-6). As Thomas Schreiner notes, "The logic seems to be that a transformed life is evidence that believers are not guilty in God's law court".[33] The key word there is 'evidence'. The transformed life is not the grounds of justification, but the evidence. God is not just concerned that we escape hell, but also that we pursue holiness.

So how is the righteous requirement of the law fully met in us?

I strongly believe in 'imputed righteousness'—that is, God graciously giving the righteousness of Christ to his people. Wonderfully, God's righteousness comes "to the one who does not work but trusts God who justifies the ungodly" (Rom 4:5). In Australia, we have a term for those who choose not to work for no good reason: 'bludger'. It's a hard word to explain, but a similar idea would be 'free loader'. But when it

---

[33] Thomas R Schreiner, *Romans*, BECNT, Baker Academic, Grand Rapids, 1998, p. 404.

comes to imputed righteousness, we should all be bludgers. Unless we are prepared to bludge on the promises of God in Christ, which come to us by grace as a gift, we will not be justified.

However, I do not think Paul is solely referring to that truth here. Through his Son, God has set us free to do what he always wanted his image-bearers to do: love God, and love others (Deut 6:4-5; Mark 12:30-31). As Paul says later in Romans, "whoever loves others has fulfilled the law" (Rom 13:8). Not surprisingly, then, love is deemed the greatest of all things; without it we are nothing, and love alone is the currency of the age to come (1 Corinthians 13).

At the cross, Christ's atoning work to pay for sins is complete. Christ's work at the cross only reaches its conclusion, however, when we love God and love each other to the glory of God the Father. This is "the obedience that comes from faith" that Paul mentioned in Romans 1:5 and 15:18, and it's for all the nations. The neglected dimension of the cross is that Christ died "that those who live should no longer live for themselves but for him who died for them and was raised again" (2 Cor 5:15).

As I mentioned, God's military-style operation to deal with the controlling power of sin involves two phases. If phase one focuses on the death of Christ, phase two focuses on the ministry of the Spirit. *God for us* becomes *God in us* to set us free. Hence, Paul writes in Romans 8:2: "…through Christ Jesus the law of the Spirit who gives life has set you free from the law of sin and death". The law that apart from the Spirit was used to produce sin and death now, in the realm of the Spirit, results in obedience.[34]

Furthermore, Romans 8:4b tells us that God condemned sin in the flesh "in order that the righteous requirement of the law might be fully met in us, who do not live according to the flesh but according to the Spirit". As Schreiner observes, "The use of the participle 'walk' shows that the concrete obedience of believers is in mind" in verse 4.[35]

Here is the fulfilment of God's great promise in the Old Testament. The finger of God, which wrote his law on two stone tablets, now writes his law on our hearts by his Holy Spirit. Through the prophet Ezekiel, God predicted that this new era was coming when he said:

> "I will give you a new heart and put a new spirit in you; I will remove from you your heart of stone and give you a heart of flesh. And I will put my Spirit in you and move you to follow my decrees and be careful to keep my laws." (Ezek 36:26-27)

---

34 It is possible that "the law of sin and death" refers to the law of Moses in the realm of the flesh (cf. Rom 4:15), while "the law of the Spirit who gives life" is the law of Christ within the sphere of the Spirit (cf. 1 Cor 9:22). In contrast to this view, however, Schreiner notes that, "Although it is difficult to be certain, the idea that the Mosaic law is intended in both uses of the word *nomos* ['law'] in verse 2 is more probable. According to this construction, the Mosaic law is in the realm either of the Holy Spirit or of the powers of sin and death. If the law is appropriated in the realm of the Spirit and by faith, then one is liberated from using the Mosaic law in such a way that leads to sin and death… Without the Spirit the law only produces death. But for those who have the Spirit the law plays a positive role" (*Romans*, p. 400).

35 Schreiner, *Romans*, p. 406; cf. John Stott, *The Message of Romans: God's Good News for the World*, BST, IVP, Leicester, 1994, p. 223.

Those of us in Christ are no longer under the condemnation that our sinful nature deserves. Instead, we are free at last to love what God loves and hate what God hates. What the law on its own could not do because of our sinful nature, God did by sending his Son and then sending his Spirit, so that we will love God and love our neighbour. As has been said, without the law of Christ, love has no eyes; without the love of Christ, the law has no heart. Or as John Stott says:

> ...the law-obedience of the people of God is so important to God that he sent his Son to die for us and his Spirit to live in us, in order to secure it. Holiness is the fruit of trinitarian grace, of the Father sending his Son into the world and his Spirit into our hearts.[36]

The work of the Spirit is to convict us of our sin and transform us from one degree of glory to the next. However, our sin sometimes smothers our understanding of the fact that God is constantly at work in our lives. The result is that we become more aware of our failures than of the profound changes God has made in us. Both are important!

Some years ago, I heard about the prayer habits of TC Hammond, former principal of Moore Theological College. At the end of each day he would pray two prayers: a prayer of confession for the sins he'd committed that day, and a prayer of thanksgiving for the good works God had accomplished in him by the Holy Spirit. He was thanking God for doing what God had promised he would do.[37]

Remember, Christ came so that we would bear fruit, not

---

36 Stott, *The Message of Romans*, p. 222.
37 I am indebted to Archbishop Glenn Davies for this story.

guilt. We are finally free to be able to fulfil the righteous requirement of the law.

Many of us who are in Christ don't pray this way or think this way for a number of reasons. It may be due to a false humility, or perhaps the result of taking the changes God has made in us for granted. I also suspect that our hesitation is because we are worried we might sound like the Pharisee who was condemned in Jesus' parable in Luke 18: "God, I thank you that I am not like other people—robbers, evildoers, adulterers—or even like this tax collector. I fast twice a week and give a tenth of all I get" (vv. 11-12). But this Pharisee was not condemned because he gave thanks to God for changing him by his Spirit; he was condemned because he confessed no sin and trusted in his own righteousness, and as a result he looked down on others.

Never become numb to the real, life-changing work of the Spirit that happens around us day by day. I'm amazed that in a culture with so many entertainment options, people turn up for church and Bible study most weeks. That is the work of the Spirit.

I'm amazed at the generosity of God's people. The wallet may be the last thing to get converted, but when it does God should be praised.

I'm amazed at the men and women who persevere in difficult marriages with joy. That is the work of the Spirit.

I remain amazed at people who put Christ first, even if it means profoundly disappointing the significant others in their life. That is the work of the Spirit.

I'm amazed at the depth of sin that some people in my church have had committed against them, and yet they have forgiven from the heart. That is the work of the Spirit.

I'm amazed at the way some saints endure horrific and ongoing chronic pain with persevering joy, resulting in hard-fought smiles.

Have no doubt: the power of sin and the flesh has its ongoing influence, but it does not have control any more.

When my church plant amalgamated with an existing (and struggling) parish, the first funeral I took was for a long-standing member of that parish. Mrs White clearly trusted in Jesus' death for her forgiveness, and she had a deep love for and commitment to the members of her church. I ended my talk at her funeral by saying: "Here lies Mrs White, a woman whose life was littered with good works. Yet she never trusted one of them for her salvation." This was the fruit of a life transformed by the Spirit.

How the Son and Spirit set me free from being an angry man

It is no surprise to know that the journey of transformation begins with an unqualified confession before God. But I can only approach the throne of grace with confidence because God is merciful in declaring that there is "no condemnation for those who are in Christ Jesus" (Rom 8:1). I've learned that I need to meditate primarily not on the law but on the cross, where Christ himself took full responsibility for my sinful anger. I can now serve God without the fear of experiencing his wrath on me, which frees me to deal with my sin honestly before God, and to not pour out my wrath on others in the process (cf. 1 John 4:17-19).

I find this often-repeated phrase very helpful: "You can't fight a sin that is not already forgiven". However, after accumulating what seems to be an endless string of ugly and painful expressions of anger, I can easily feel stuck. I face the constant temptation to believe two lies: that God is sick of hearing me confess another of my many angry outbursts; and that I can't change and I will never change.

But the realization that I am 'in Christ' profoundly affected me. I can't make God angry any more. "Really?" I remember thinking to myself, "Is that right? Am I allowed to say it that boldly?" Yes! What else does it mean for us to say that there is "no condemnation for those who are in Christ Jesus"? Failure to claim this truth is to deny the significance of the once-for-all death of my Saviour.

It's true that I can grieve the Spirit, who will redeem my body and soul (cf. Eph 4:30). But I live every moment in a state of grace, where I am set free from the law of sin and death to be what God has called me to be. And not wanting to grieve the Spirit is its own motivation to say no to sinful displays of anger.

The days of going for a walk and holding hands with anger as my friend are over—and for good reason. Unrighteous anger kills those who are on the receiving end of it, and those who wish to be friends with it. This is where my journey to terminate unrighteous anger in my life begins and ends. It is why I want to side with God against my anger in regular confession, rather than siding with my anger against God.

4
The power of the Spirit to transform
Romans 8:5-8

⁵ Those who live according to the flesh have their minds set on what the flesh desires; but **those who live in accordance with the Spirit have their minds set on what the Spirit desires.** ⁶ The mind governed by the flesh is death, but the mind governed by the Spirit is life and peace. ⁷ The mind governed by the flesh is hostile to God; it does not submit to God's law, nor can it do so. ⁸ Those who are in the realm of the flesh cannot please God. (Rom 8:5-8)

Religion wants to put a new suit on the man. But God sent his Son and his Spirit to put a new man in the suit. Even though God the Father initiated his great plan of salvation, and even though his Son obediently lived the life we should have lived and died taking full responsibility for our sins, not one person would have responded and been saved if God had not sent his Spirit. The Spirit of God is absolutely indispensable to God's solution to the problem of our sin. So we now turn to further explore the power of the Spirit to transform those in Christ.

Diets don't work. I am living proof, because I have been dieting since I was 12. I have felt fat since I was 5. Being told I was a 'fatty-boom-sticks' and having man boobs at age 11 didn't help. I dropped the weight off around ages 15-23, when the opposite sex proved a great motivation. But the moment I was married at age 24, I started putting the kilos back on. It started with a honeymoon gift of chocolate-coated macadamia nuts.

Will I ever change?

There is a part of me that wants to change for good reasons. I am inspired by a couple of guys at my church who have lost a lot of weight. But they lost it in two very different ways. One of them, George, lost it by having two-thirds of his stomach removed. It was major elective surgery. I asked George how he justified the decision, and he humorously quoted the words of Jesus: "If your right hand causes you to stumble, cut it off and throw it away" (Matt 5:30). The other man at church, Joe, lost the same amount of weight by following a disciplined program of healthy eating and regular exercise. While I have concerns about the surgical solution, I have more hope that it will be the winner.

I wish the Christian life could be like a one-off operation that would simply take away the urge to sin. I would love to have spiritual surgery that meant I don't have to engage in the daily battle of denying myself or dealing with the fallout from my many failures. I am not talking here about dieting, but about something much harder and much more important: the daily battle with sin.

It all raises the question: Is any real change possible? Can real change be permanent? Or is the promise of transformation simply a mirage?

Romans 8 has much to say on this issue as it focuses on the ministry of the Spirit, with 20 explicit references to the third person of the Trinity.[38] This is very significant, given that there are only four references to the Spirit in chapters 1-7, and there will only be eight more in chapters 9-16.[39] In verses 5-8 of chapter 8, Paul begins to show us how it is that the Spirit makes real, lasting change a possibility for the Christian.

Living according to the flesh

These verses offer a stark contrast between those in the Spirit and those in the flesh. You really see the power of God's Spirit to change when you realize what he has to work with!

This is not about a believer who at times lives in the realm of the Spirit and at other times lives in the realm of the flesh. The difference between the two realms is absolute. A person is either in one or the other. It's like being pregnant: you either are or you aren't. You can't be half pregnant, and you can't be half 'in the flesh' and half 'in the Spirit'. If you don't have the Spirit, you're not a Christian. It's as simple as that.

---

38 In Romans 8 there are 21 occurrences of the word *pneuma* (which means 'Spirit'—but which can also be translated 'breath' or 'wind' in certain contexts). However, one of the references (in verse 16) is to our spirit. This count does not include any pronouns for which *pneuma* might be the referent. (I am indebted to Matt Olliffe for this insight.)
39 Rom 1:9; 2:29; 5:5; 7:6; 9:1; 11:8; 12:11; 14:17; 15:13, 16, 19, 30.

Let's start by looking at those whose minds are set on what the sinful nature requires. Paul begins by saying, "Those who live according to the flesh have their minds set on what the flesh desires" (8:5a). As John Murray observes, "to set one's mind on the desires of either the flesh or the Spirit is to make them absorbing objects of thought, interest, affection and purpose".[40] This is a powerful description of the mind controlled by the flesh, or the sinful nature.

To say that someone is 'in the flesh' is another way of saying that they are without the Spirit of God and without Christ. In verse 6, the mind governed by the sinful nature is described in one word: death. Look how starkly Paul puts it: "The mind governed by the flesh is death". We were by nature spiritually dead, resulting in physical death and culminating in the 'second death'—our eternal separation from God.

But this is not just passive rebellion, for in verse 7 we read that the sinful mindset is "hostile to God". Without the Spirit of Christ, we are at war with God. That is why Christ died for us "while we were God's enemies" (5:10)—we turned the one who created us into an opponent. Without the Spirit, we refuse to submit to God's law. We deliberately oppose God's will.

Notice also that Paul says not just that we *don't* submit to God's law, but also that we *can't* submit: "The mind governed by the flesh… does not submit to God's law, nor can it do so" (8:7). It is nothing less than impossible for those who live in the flesh to render obedience to the law of God.

How is it, then, that there are billions of humans who

---

[40] John Murray, *The Collected Writings of John Murray*, vol. 1, *The Claims of Truth*, Banner of Truth, Edinburgh, 1976, p. 285.

have no regard for Jesus but have very high ethical standards in all kinds of areas, from social justice to family values?

First, Jesus himself said to his own disciples, "If you then, though you are evil, know how to give good gifts to your children, how much more will your Father in heaven give the Holy Spirit to those who ask him" (Luke 11:13). So it is possible to do good and to be kind to your children, and yet be certified by Jesus himself as 'evil'.

Second, critical to understanding God's law is recognizing that it begins with loving God with all your heart, and that God is unapologetically jealous for our loyalty. So begin the Ten Commandments: "You shall have no other gods before me" (Exod 20:3). Choosing to obey five of the Ten Commandments does not stop me from being an enemy of God. I can love my wife in many different ways—from listening to her pain to providing breakfast in bed each morning—but if I am engaging in a sexual relationship with another person then I am her enemy, no matter what I tell her or myself. It is no different with God.

Even in a home where the family practises sincere religion, there can be a resistance to God's will that politely refashions him in ways that are self-serving rather than God-pleasing. Paul calls it exchanging the truth of God for a lie, and worshipping and serving the creation rather than the Creator (Rom 1:23). The created things that we love are generally good things in themselves. For example, every parent should obviously love their children. The problem comes when a parent loves their children more than they love Jesus. I remember asking Gina, a dying Italian mother who had recently accepted Christ, if she could look her two adult daughters in the eye and say, "I love you girls so much, but

I love Jesus even more". She did, and I knew she was truly born again.

But as Romans 8:8 reminds us, the mind controlled by the sinful nature cannot please God. It's not just that we break God's laws; we break his heart. It's always personal with God. That's why Jesus can look even his disciples in the eye and call them 'evil'. Yes, we can all do good, but underneath lies a heart that fails to fully love and honour God.

The classic contemporary test case for the power of the sinful nature is the internet. For the first time in the history of world, humanity has unrestricted access to whatever information or image it desires. And what does humanity want? It wants large doses of hard-core pornography that treats adults and children as mere objects to be used for one's pleasure. The Bible's diagnosis of human nature, left to itself, is humbling: we will not and *cannot* please God. It's often said that we can do whatever we set our minds to, but Romans 8:8 demolishes such human pride.

The apostle Paul calls those in Christ to renew their mind as the basis of their total life's worship to God (12:1-2). However, Romans 8 takes us one step back, telling us that our nature determines our thinking, which in turn determines our behaviour and destiny.[41] We have either a nature shared with Adam, or a nature renewed by the Spirit. One leads to death; the other leads to life.

Preacher and writer Phillip Jensen tells the story of a man who came to his church and told him that he thought the

---

41 "The meaning surely is not that people are like this because they think like this, although that is partly true, but that they think like this because they are like this" (Stott, *The Message of Romans*, p. 223).

Bible's view of human nature was just too bleak. So Phillip gave the man a challenge: "Be good for just one week". The man agreed, confident he could achieve the goal. A week later he returned to church, a little sheepish. "How did you go?" asked Phillip. The man felt it was an unrealistic expectation because it was just too open-ended. So Phillip agreed to limit the challenge to just one area: "Try not lying for one week". "That, I can do!" boasted the man. A week later he returned, claiming that the challenge simply wasn't fair. "Why not? Didn't you agree to it?" The man confessed, "Yes. But I've just started working as a real estate agent."

I'm always more optimistic about human nature when I think in the abstract. However, when I think in terms of specifics, I'm not so hopeful.

Living according to the Spirit

What about those who are controlled by the Spirit?

They are transformed from being hostile towards God to being friends with God. In the words of Jesus, it is a transformation from death to life (John 5:24). The mindset controlled by the Spirit is captured in two words: 'life' and 'peace' (Rom 8:6). One woman in our church who came to Christ from a Muslim background described being a Christian this way: "I now feel comfortable in my own skin". She was experiencing the implications of being at peace with God (Rom 5:1) —*shalom*!

What sociologists, social engineering, and strong caring families cannot do, God did: it is the power of the Spirit that creates a living obedience. As a result, the phrase "they will never change" must never be on the lips of Christians. Giving up on people is another way of giving up on God's work through his Spirit.

The conversion of Saul (Acts 9:1-31) is one classic example of how dramatically a person can change when confronted by the Lord Jesus and the power of his Spirit. Saul, who was also called Paul and who wrote the book of Romans, openly confessed to being the worst of sinners (1 Tim 1:15). We might say he was the Osama bin Laden of the first century. No-one was expecting his transformation, and it took some time for his fellow believers to trust him. Yet by God's grace, he went from persecutor to persecuted, from opposing Jesus to proclaiming Jesus as the Son of God and Saviour of the world.

The power of the Spirit prevents us from giving up on anyone.

I recall a conversation with a man who was engaged in a life of serial adultery and reckless gambling before coming to Christ. His wife mentioned how she had often prayed that God would change his behaviour. But she came to understand that she should have prayed for God to change his *heart*. He needed a Spirit-led regeneration, not mere behavioural reform. He needed to be born again, which is another way of saying he needed to be born of the Spirit (John 3:1-8). Once that happened, he was a new man, and the adulteries and gambling eventually disappeared.

But we are left with a conundrum. We know of those 'in the flesh' who, let's face it, are much nicer people than those 'in the Spirit'. How does one explain this paradox? There are several things to say.

First, as Tim Keller says, Christians "should expect to find nonbelievers who are much nicer, kinder, wiser, and better than they are. Why? Christian believers are not accepted by God because of their moral performance, wisdom, or virtue, but because of Christ's work on their behalf."[42]

Second, God's common grace means that he is at work in the world among his image-bearers, whether they are 'in the Spirit' or 'in the flesh'. Proverbs teaches us that this is a moral universe, and a non-Christian is capable of working out a degree of wise living even without the fear of the Lord. This is the gift of God, which restrains evil and allows this world to be liveable. Even when God hands humanity over to its sin (Rom 1:24, 26, 28), it is not a complete abandonment; it is not hell. That is why we thank God each time we see kind deeds performed by those who don't know Christ.

Third, those in the Spirit do not all start their new life in the Spirit from the same place. Each of us was dealt a different hand under the providence of God. For example, some grew up in abusive homes, others in loving and secure family environments. That is one of the reasons Jesus says, "From everyone who has been given much, much will be demanded" (Luke 12:48). We measure the journey of the saints from whence they come.

Fourth, not only do we all start our Christian walk in different places; not every Christian is at the same stage of their walk. Some are new Christians, still in the spiritual nursery, saying and doing dumb things. Others have been walking in the Spirit for many years and have matured like a good wine, making them quick to listen and slow to speak.

Fifth, the issue needs to be viewed across generations.

---

[42] Timothy Keller, *The Reason for God: Belief in an Age of Skepticism*, Penguin, New York, 2008, p. 19.

There are those who have come to Christ from cultures and family lines that are profoundly anti-Christian at many levels. It may take several generations to deal with these issues, but the Spirit will do his work over time.

Sixth, those who are in the Spirit but lack much fruit may need to be gently confronted in love, not just tolerated within the church of God. Regardless of one's background, God expects that the saints grow in their love for each other more and more. Yes, the Spirit works in all believers to change them, but we are still commanded to "keep in step with the Spirit" (Gal 5:25). Sometimes we are stubborn and hard-hearted, which means we can be slow to experience the kind of change that the Spirit is working to bring about. What doesn't help is when the church fails to teach that while Christians are only saved by grace and not by works, they are also saved to do good works. It doesn't help that, at times, we neglect the grace of church discipline—a grace that God gives us to enable us to be what he has called us to be (1 Cor 5:5-12).

Seventh, those in the flesh may exhibit wonderful characteristics outwardly, but God judges the heart. Right behaviour for the wrong reason is still sin—just a more sophisticated and socially acceptable version of it. As we saw earlier, it's possible to do the right things for the wrong reasons, not for God-honouring reasons.

One man who came to Christ told me that he would never lie as a non-Christian. This shocked me, given that before I came to Christ my whole life was a lie. When I asked him why he didn't lie, he said, "It just made me feel good to tell the truth!" This man recognized that telling the truth was the right thing to do, but he did so with no regard at all for

God and his glory. While in the flesh, his thinking was still futile. But now, in the Spirit, he told the truth for Jesus' sake.

A number of important pastoral issues flow once we understand the significance of the promised life lived in the Spirit.

As we share the awesome news that Jesus is Lord, we need to be aware that our non-believing listeners are already anticipating the cost of commitment and the changes involved if they accept Christ. Many are mindful of their own long-standing moral breaches and their weak will, even if only subconsciously. This can make the idea of following Jesus as Lord seem like just one more case of being set up for a fall. Before each person lies a significant cost if they decide to say yes to Jesus and no to sin—whether it's greed, or pride, or ungodly sexual attraction, or various forms of addiction, or any number of other temptations that will be enormously difficult to resist.

For this reason, it's critical that in preaching Christ we also point to the promise of the Spirit, who will enable people to change—and who will enable them to *want* to change and be more like their Lord. God will not abandon them to their fleshly nature, for when they come to Christ they are in the Spirit and the Spirit is in them.

It's equally important to understand that life in the Spirit is not a straightforward upward trajectory in which we gain one victory over another. The Christian life is messy, and the reality is that not every day will be better than the one before (although this should always be our aim).

It's easy to condemn others or to assume that they're

disqualified from being in Christ based on what we perceive about sin in their life. But we all need to show one another the same patience that our Father in heaven shows to us, especially when we witness a brother or sister in Christ repeatedly fall into the same sin. Such a person was once often referred to as the 'backslider'.

Careful balance is needed when dealing with professing Christians who are caught in sin. On the one hand, it's possible to 'backslide' and yet still be a genuine child of God. The allure of sin may deceive and capture us for a time, but those who are filled with the Spirit will, on some level, hate their own sin (even while they're living in the midst of sin). No-one whose mind is "governed by the Spirit" can ever truly accept rebellion against God, and so the 'backslider' lives in a certain kind of agony. But those who are chosen by God will eventually heed the warnings that are sprinkled throughout the Bible. If we meet someone who claims to follow Christ but is living in persistent sin with zero desire to change, the alarm bells should start ringing loud and clear.

At the same time, as we'll see in chapter 11, God will glorify all those he has chosen, and we are entitled to experience a powerful sense of assurance as we remember these promises and see God at work in our lives. Through his Son and his Spirit, God has done what people could not do on their own. He will generate newfound desires that were not there before. God is not only *for us*, but he is also working *in us* to do his will. God will complete the work he began in us.

Change can happen, and change does happen—but it's messy.

The fleshly sin of pride behind my anger

A couple of years ago, I read about a man who stole a 49-tonne bulldozer and demolished his ex-friend's house, boat, and four cars. As I read the article, I was reminded of Proverbs 14:17: "A quick-tempered person does foolish things".

I still remember the first time I was seriously convicted about my anger. I was preparing a sermon from Matthew 5:21-22 on how anger and murder spring from the same heart, and how God takes both very seriously. While I was writing the talk, I remembered a time years before when my son James was about five years old. It was in the early days of our church plant, and I was foolishly working too hard with too many late nights. James innocently woke me up early one morning, asking me to put on his favourite TV show. All I remember was being very angry that he had woken me up. While I apologised to James soon after, it was years later as I was writing the sermon that I typed these words: "I murdered my son that day". The memory still makes me want to cry. I knew I was forgiven by God, but I also knew I was being convicted by God's tender Spirit.

It's easy to see the foolishness and evil of things like physical violence and verbal abuse, which are obvious targets for spiritual assassination. However, less obvious sins like passive-aggressive sulking and sarcasm also need to be put to death. These subtle sins are perhaps, in some ways, the most insidious culprits of all, simply because they don't appear so evil. Let's face it: sarcasm is, for many, a middle-class virtue. But like a slow-growing cancer, sins like this can subtly destroy relationships without a punch being thrown or a voice being raised.

I recall a couple coming to speak to me after a sermon in which I shared my struggle with anger. They gently said to me, "Ray, have you ever thought that behind your anger was pride?" I faked humility to them. And I was too proud at the time to admit this to myself, but they were right. In the fullness of time, God's Spirit used that conversation to help me rethink my struggle with anger.

Augustine was right when he said that pride is the mother of all sins. My anger betrays a 'spirit of demandingness'. I require the world to operate on my terms and on my agenda, with me at the centre of the universe. James captures this demanding spirit that fuels anger and conflict: "What causes fights and quarrels among you? Don't they come from your desires that battle within you? You desire but do not have, so you kill. You covet but you cannot get what you want, so you quarrel and fight" (Jas 4:1-2a).

Some schools of psychology view anger as a secondary emotion, with the primary emotion being hurt. I fully agree. Anger seeks to either punish the person who is hurting us, or protect us from further hurt. But behind this psychological insight, the fleshly sin of pride remains. Pride desires and demands that we be treated properly, and woe betide anyone who crosses our path. There is also a form of pride that refuses to be vulnerable or to speak openly about our hurt. The result is that we demonize the ones who wound us.

It's also worth noting that anger lacks basic wisdom in the sense that it's very hard for others to hear our pain when it comes gift-wrapped in the barbed wire of anger. It's both wrong and dumb.

I remember a time when I was angry with my wife, Sandy. Behind the anger was a deep hurt at something she said (to be honest, I can't even remember what it was—isn't that so often the case?). She would never have known of my hurt because all she received was a blast from her supposedly disrespected husband. My anger kept us apart and made me quietly demonize Sandy. Eventually I shared my hurt, which quickly brought us back together. But what delayed me in sharing my hurt was simply the pride that wanted to avoid being vulnerable. The work of the Spirit has included having me slowly learn to share a hurt with gentleness, rather than expressing it with a sinful burst of aggressiveness.

Anger is one of my struggles. What is yours? Where is God's Spirit pointing out to you how your pride has reared its ugly head in your life? How might the Spirit of God be driving out the fleshly sin of pride?

5

The presence of the Spirit
Romans 8:9-14

⁹ You, however, are not in the realm of the flesh but are in the realm of the Spirit, if indeed the Spirit of God lives in you. And if anyone does not have the Spirit of Christ, they do not belong to Christ. ¹⁰ But if Christ is in you, then even though your body is subject to death because of sin, the Spirit gives life because of righteousness. ¹¹ And if the Spirit of him who raised Jesus from the dead is living in you, he who raised Christ from the dead will also give life to your mortal bodies because of his Spirit who lives in you.

¹² Therefore, brothers and sisters, we have an obligation—but it is not to the flesh, to live according to it. ¹³ For if you live according to the flesh, you will die; but if by the Spirit you put to death the misdeeds of the body, you will live.

¹⁴ For those who are led by the Spirit of God are the children of God. (Rom 8:9-14)

We've all had those houseguests from hell. One visitor who stayed for three long weeks never changed out of his pyjamas, took his laptop everywhere (including to the dining table at meal times), ate us out of house and home while never sharing any of his own snacks, couldn't muster a 'thank you', and then complained about Australia until we finally showed him the door. As a result, I'm now just a little fussy about who I live with or who lives with me in my home.

In contrast, God in his grace will allow undeserving sinners like us to enter into his perfect home forever, through Christ—and now, while we wait, he also comes to dwell in us by his Spirit. The presence of God's Spirit living in a believer is one of the awesome privileges of being a Christian.

God's promise to dwell with his people is a consistent theme in the Bible. It was expressed in the garden of Eden when God walked with Adam "in the cool of the day" (Gen 3:8). God promised to be with Abram (and his offspring) as he left his father's world for the land God prepared (Gen 12:1-5). God guaranteed he would dwell with Israel in the Promised Land, and more specifically in the tabernacle and later in the temple (e.g. Exod 25:8-9; Lev 26:12). God promised that after the exile, he would lead his people back into the Promised Land (e.g. Jer 29:10-11).

In the fullness of time, God came in person, became flesh, and made his dwelling among us in the person of Jesus (John 1:14). In so doing, God permanently sided with us humans. Jesus' last words before he ascended back into heaven were, "And surely I am with you always, to the very end of the age" (Matt 28:20). The ongoing presence of Jesus is now fulfilled in the gift of the person of the Holy Spirit given both to individuals (1 Cor 6:19) and to the church (1 Cor 3:16). The Bible's final vision is of God dwelling with humans in the new creation, where they will see his face (Rev 21:3, 22; 22:4).

The great privilege, often unappreciated by many believers, is that God through his Spirit doesn't just visit you at the point of conversion with a "Just passing, thought I'd drop in". He comes to make his permanent home within your inner being, turning your own unique body into his holy temple (1 Cor 6:19). The Spirit does not simply kickstart your life in Christ and then leave the rest of your journey up to you. He permanently dwells within you.

The mark of a Christian: the Spirit living within

> You, however, are not in the realm of the flesh but are in the realm of the Spirit, if indeed the Spirit of God lives in you. (Rom 8:9a)

Not once, but three times in Romans 8:9-11 we are told that the Spirit lives in those united to Christ. Paul has no doubt that all those who are in Christ have the Spirit. The word 'if' in verse 9 could also be translated 'since': you are in the realm of the Spirit *since* the Spirit of God lives in you.

If you are a believer, one of God's special gifts to you is that he has made you his dwelling place. What was said of the tabernacle and the temple in the Old Testament is now said of you. Whether or not you have the Spirit determines whether or not you belong to Christ. Paul states this point positively in the first half of verse 9, and then reinforces it by saying the same thing negatively in the second half of the verse: "And if anyone does not have the Spirit of Christ, they do not belong to Christ" (8:9b).

The Bible typically says that if you have Christ, you have the Spirit. Normally the language in the Scriptures is something like 'Believe/repent in the Lord Jesus, and you will receive the Holy Spirit' (e.g. Acts 2:38; Gal 3:2; Eph 1:13). Here, however, the order is reversed. Either way, there is a very tight connection between having the Spirit and having Christ.

This close link between the Spirit, Christ and God is seen in the way Paul sometimes uses these words interchangeably. Notice, for example, how his language is fluid in verse 9, moving between 'the Spirit', 'the Spirit of God', 'the Spirit of Christ', and 'Christ'. To have the Spirit dwelling in us is to have Christ dwelling in us (without denying that there is an important distinction between the persons of the Trinity).[43] You can't belong to Christ and not have the Spirit. Equally, you can't have the Spirit and not belong to Christ.

This knocks two classic errors on the head. The first error is the idea that you can have a 'Spiritless' Christianity. Some claim that you can believe in Christ, submit to him and receive forgiveness, and still not receive his Spirit or be baptized in the Spirit. But Paul is crystal clear: if you don't have the Spirit, you don't belong to Christ (1 Cor 12:3, 12-13). If you have Christ, you have the Spirit. The Spirit is both the cause and the consequence of our faith in Christ. The Spirit

---

[43] The word 'person' can refer to humans, to angels and to God himself. It refers to a being with personality and distinct identity. (Sorry, pet lovers—dogs and cats are not included!) That's why we speak about 'one God' but 'three persons' when it comes to the Trinity.

creates faith in Christ, and with that faith comes the full measure of the Spirit of Christ.

The second error to be corrected is the idea of a 'Christless' spirituality. This view claims that you can have a true spirituality without accepting Christ as the eternal and unique Son of God. But it is a misdirected spirituality that fails to submit to Christ as Lord. The Lord Jesus is not just the best of many options; he is the only option, and the only way to the Father.

The modern catchcry is "I'm spiritual, but I'm not religious". Many have broken free not just from institutional Christianity but also from biblical Christianity, and yet they still want to lay claim to something beyond a purely materialist worldview. 'Spiritual' can simply mean something ineffable—a feeling of wholeness and surpassing wonder. But as Ed Welch rightly puts it, "Today you can be spiritual, it would seem, if you believe in your left shoe".[44] Yet Scripture insists that without faith in the biblical Christ, any form of spirituality is ultimately a false spirituality.

The Spirit gives life to our mortal bodies

But if Christ is in you, then even though your body is subject to death because of sin, the Spirit gives life because of righteousness. And if the Spirit of him who raised Jesus from the dead is living in you, he who raised Christ from the dead will also give life to your mortal bodies because of his Spirit who lives in you. (Rom 8:10-11)

---

44 Edward T Welch, *When People Are Big and God Is Small: Overcoming Peer Pressure, Co-dependency and the Fear of Man*, P&R Publishing, Phillipsburg, NJ, 1997, p. 85.

The presence of the Spirit in us brings a quota of guarantees. What the Spirit did to Jesus at his resurrection is what the Spirit will do to you when you die, and what he will do is raise your body to life.

It's not going to be like the dream I had as a teenager, where I was at my own funeral. Even though I was very much aware that I was in the coffin, I could see and hear everything. At first I was really enjoying the experience. I felt so loved as my family and friends were all present, all saying some very kind things about me. I didn't want it to end.

But as the coffin was being lowered into the ground, I saw the faces of my loved ones looking down on me, and a sense of dread came upon me. The horror of death struck me when I saw my family and friends turn their backs to go home, and I was left behind, feeling very much alone in that grave. I had such a strong sense that death marked the end of life and the end of relationships. In that dream, death had won.

But the resurrection of Christ turns that nightmare on its head. As surely as the Spirit raised Christ from the dead, so he will raise those who are in Christ.

Here again we encounter the life-giving language of assurance. The certainty of my future resurrection hinges on the certainty of Christ's resurrection. The same Spirit is involved in both operations. The Spirit that raised Jesus from death now personally dwells within us—hence the guarantee that the same Spirit who enables me to say 'no' to sin is the same Spirit who is going to say 'yes' to me when he hands out new bodies on the last day.

All of this carries some extraordinary implications.

Our obligation to live according to the Spirit

> Therefore, brothers and sisters, we have an obligation—but it is not to the flesh, to live according to it. (Rom 8:12)

The Bible gives us multiple reasons to do what is right. One of those reasons is that we have a sense of obligation. A debt is owed. There is an obligation not just toward the Father and the Son, but also to the Holy Spirit, reinforcing the fact that the Spirit is a person in his own right.

Many Christians grasp that we have an obligation to God the Father, because he initiated the plan of salvation. He did not withhold his one and only Son, who came in the likeness of sinful flesh to be a sin offering for us (v. 3). Many Christians also understand that we have an obligation to the Lord Jesus, because he executes the plan of salvation by giving himself up for us even while we were certified enemies. But perhaps the most neglected motivation for obedience given in the Bible is in connection with the Spirit. This obligation is clearly implied in the contrast between flesh and Spirit in this section. When Paul says, "we have an obligation—but it is not to the flesh" (v. 12), he wants us to see that we *do* have an obligation to the Spirit.

We have an obligation to the Spirit because he applies God's plan of salvation, both now and continuing on to the last day. He is the Holy Spirit, the "Spirit of holiness" (1:4). We have an obligation to let the Holy Spirit live up to his name in us.

The Spirit who dwells within the believer is also going to raise us to life on the last day. We owe our resurrection life to the Spirit of God, who makes his home in our hearts. In contrast, we owe nothing to the one who tries to kill us, which is what the flesh (sinful nature) will do. The fact of the matter is that if you live according to the sinful nature, you will die. The flesh enslaves its victims and renders them powerless to approach God, placing them under a sentence of condemnation and death. As John Stott so helpfully puts it, "How can we possess life and court death?"[45]

The Spirit, however, personally dwells within, wooing your human spirit and making you alive to God. His pleasure becomes your joy. And the same Spirit will be there as your body is reclaimed from the dead and transformed into the same kind of body as the glorified Lord Jesus, who ascended into heaven (Phil 3:20-21). We owe him big time!

Putting to death misdeeds of the body

> For if you live according to the flesh, you will die; but if by the Spirit you put to death the misdeeds of the body, you will live.
>
> For those who are led by the Spirit of God are the children of God. (Rom 8:13-14)

How will you know whether a person is led (or indwelt) by the Spirit?

One of the chief marks, apart from confessing Jesus as Lord (1 Cor 12:1-3), is an active commitment to putting to death the misdeeds of the body. Every Christian who is born of the Spirit reports a deep desire to want to obey God, even if sinful desires still lurk. The sins that gave pleasure now

---

[45] Stott, *The Message of Romans*, p. 227.

begin to leave a bad taste in one's soul. It truly is a miracle.

Romans 8 offers us a healthy realism regarding the Christian life. There is no promise of perfection this side of glory, or of achieving heaven on earth. Nor am I forced to pretend that life is about having one endless victory after another. The battle required to put sin to death is ongoing and painful. However, it's easy to let the sins we are still battling overshadow the work of God's Spirit in making us alive to God. As has been said:

> I may not always be what God wants me to be.
> I may not be what others want me to be.
> And I may not be what I want to be.
> But I know that I am not what I used to be.

None of us, no matter our background, is what we once were. It does you good to recall what you are by nature, even if you came to Christ on your mother's knee and can't recall a 'before' story. Just imagine if God were to withdraw his Spirit from you right now. What difference would it make? Make a list of the things that would change, then thank God for the transformation he is making and sustaining in your life.

But while Paul offers great hope by pointing to the Spirit's work in us, he does not ignore the present tension that every Christian faces. Even if we have the Spirit of Christ in us and our spirit is alive, nevertheless our bodies are "subject to death because of sin" (Rom 8:10). We have not yet been given our heavenly, glorified bodies. In our spirit we want to obey God, but we cart around bodies that sin, that will get sick and die. The flesh does not control your body, but it still influences your body. And this tension will not get resolved until your body is resurrected.

The Spirit-led life is one of repentance, not pessimism. We are called to become assassins of sin. This is not unlike Jesus' message in the Sermon on the Mount. Our Lord did not say, "If your right hand causes you to stumble, get a manicure". Jesus said, "If your right hand causes you to stumble, cut it off and throw it away" (Matt 5:30). This shocking language calls us to take radical steps to get rid of sinful patterns.

Reflecting on Paul's description of love being patient (or 'long-suffering') in 1 Corinthians 13:4, John Piper made the following comment:

> If I am to be like this, something in me must die. My strong craving for a trouble-free life must die. My need for an uninterrupted schedule must die. My demandingness that frustrations and interference get out of my way must die.[46]

We are to view the Christian life as a war. Our spirit is alive, but our body is dead. We are not civilians; we are soldiers engaging with a savage enemy, and its name is sin. There can be no compromise!

Martyn Lloyd-Jones captures the journey of putting sin to death. Rather than involving repression or pretense, the opposite is required. Lloyd-Jones says we have to "pull [sin] out, look at it, denounce it, hate it for what it is; then you have really dealt with it".[47] To put it another way, the coming of the Spirit creates a newfound hate in our heart. As Paul

---

46 John Piper, 'Dying as a Means of Loving, Part 2', *Desiring God*, 25 June 1995 (viewed 14 April 2017): www.desiringgod.org/messages/dying-as-a-means-of-loving-part-2.
47 Lloyd-Jones, *The Sons of God*, p. 143.

says in Romans 12: "Hate what is evil; cling to what is good" (v. 9).

Take time now to think of that one area of your life where you constantly fall into sin. Who do you blame for that sin? Why is that sin so grievous to God? God is telling the truth when he promises that we will never be put in a situation where we are tempted beyond what we can bear (1 Cor 10:13). This means that when we fail, our only comeback is confession. We truly have no excuse, because God has sufficiently empowered us to resist every temptation by his Spirit. Whether I did things I should not have done (sins of commission), or whether I did not do what I should have done (sins of omission), I have no excuse.

And yet God has not abandoned me.

Two things remain to be said.

First, God does not expect us to fight the battle against sin without him. In fact, we *cannot* do it without the empowering work of his Spirit. That's why we praise him for giving us his Spirit. You are not alone in your struggle against sin! Take time to consciously remind yourself of the empowering presence of the Spirit dwelling within you.

But, second, God does not bring change without our involvement. We are to actively and wholeheartedly put sin to death. In this sense, we are not meant to 'let go and let God'. As Andy, a former youth pastor at my church, liked to say: sanctification (the process of becoming like Christ) is not like a rowboat where it's all you; nor is it like a powerboat where you sit back and do nothing. It's more like a yacht, where you and the wind work together, responding to the wind's direction and energy.

God expects a life of repentance. The warning in

Romans 8:13 ("if you live according to the flesh, you will die") is not for those who are struggling yet trying hard to obey, but for those who refuse to enter the battle with sin and surrender to the flesh. It's not the many defeats that will lead to certain death, but rather the consistent refusal to do battle with sin.

Just when you think you have been beaten again (and I know we feel this way often), hear the call of the Spirit! The normal Christian life is about constantly getting up, denying yourself, taking up your cross, and following Jesus. And each new battle begins with the word of grace: "There is now no condemnation for those who are in Christ Jesus" (Rom 8:1). We should never tire of saying "I'm sorry" to God, and God never tires of hearing our confession, nor of assuring us of his acceptance. Don't let Satan make you think otherwise.

The battle against sin takes place from *within* the family of God. Unless you understand this, your battle will be in vain. As we will see, our struggles against sin (including our many failures) do not occur within a courtroom before a judge, but within a family before a dad who will not reject us. And thanks be to God, the Spirit who gave life to all creation now gives new life to those in Christ. We are now able, at last, to please God. This is the result of being born again. What God said of his one and only Son he now says of you: "This is my Son, whom I love; with him I am well pleased" (Matt 3:17).

Letting the Spirit transform the believer and heal others

Proverbs 27:4 states that "Anger is cruel and fury overwhelming". It crushes those around us and ignores just how much God values them.

Some time ago, I ended a talk at a men's conference by challenging each man to invite feedback from their family on what it's like to be on the receiving end of their anger. Some weeks after the conference, I received an email from Yi An Neoh. I share it here with his permission and blessing. May this Spirit-transformed life inspire you as it inspired me.

> I've been a Christian for over 30 years. ... As I reflected on the anger I showed to my own family, I realized the truth of one of Ray's statements, "Your anger is always worse than the thing you're angry at", and came also to the realization that my 'justified' anger was actually a vain attempt to take over God's job in protecting others, but mainly myself.
>
> After the talk, I made up my mind to meet this issue head on and take responsibility for my anger. I published a post on Facebook so that I'd be held accountable to my friends and wider community.
>
> Later on, I sat my family down and asked them what it was like for them when I lost my temper. One of my children said that it made them "feel afraid", another said "it makes me want to run away" and sometimes it was like "walking on eggshells".
>
> It was very humbling to do but I knew I had to do it and not give my flesh any more excuses. I repented in front of them and asked them each individually

for their forgiveness. My family prayed for me and we all wept (except my youngest child!!). One of my daughters prayed and thanked God for the courage I'd been given to confront this issue. This experience has drawn me even closer to my family, and them to me. Even in three short weeks, I've noticed a difference in my relationships, especially with my middle daughter.

God does not promise to bring change without our involvement. It is clear that God's Spirit convicted Yi An as he placed himself under God's word, and yet Yi An cooperated with the Spirit's prompting by his active obedience. His response was not just remorse and private confession to God, important as both are. He took active steps to put right that which was wrong, by seeking to find out the impact of his behaviour on his family, and then speaking to them in a meaningful way about the specific nature of the damage he caused. He even made himself accountable through a public post on Facebook.

I shared his story with my congregation in a church-wide email. One woman, Anna, responded as follows:

I was deeply impacted by the story you told on Sunday, regarding the Chinese man who suffered with unhealthy expressions of anger. I too struggle with anger and fear when I try to control and protect a situation, rather than letting God hold the reins, and it often ends with me venting these emotions in unhelpful ways.

Yi An Neoh's story influenced my actions and interactions throughout the week. I have confessed my sin to Jesus, of not trusting his loving and substantial protection, and have pleaded with him to help me be vulnerable and trusting, and let him take over when I cannot. I also had a very honest conversation with my husband about this deficit. Whilst I found it confronting, it holds me accountable and has enriched our relationship and my prayer life.

6

The Spirit of sonship
Romans 8:14-17

¹⁴ For those who are led by the Spirit of God are the children of God. ¹⁵ The Spirit you received does not make you slaves, so that you live in fear again; rather, **the Spirit you received brought about your adoption to sonship.** And by him we cry, "Abba, Father." ¹⁶ The Spirit himself testifies with our spirit that we are God's children. ¹⁷ Now if we are children, then we are heirs—heirs of God and co-heirs with Christ, if indeed we share in his sufferings in order that we may also share in his glory. (Rom 8:14-17)

Based on what we've already learned in Romans 8, there is so much to be thankful for when we consider the person and work of the Spirit. The power of the Spirit leaves us optimistic as we engage in the battle with sin. We can make progress, and it is right to expect change. The presence of the Spirit gives us comfort that we are not alone in our struggle. He brings us out of the realm of the flesh and of hostility towards God, and brings us into the realm of the Spirit, which is "life and peace" (Rom 8:6).

Personally, however, I think the greatest privilege of having the Spirit is that we become children of God, adopted into his eternal family. It now pleases us to please our Father.

> The Spirit you received does not make you slaves, so that you live in fear again; rather, the Spirit you received brought about your adoption to sonship. And by him we cry, "Abba, Father." (v. 15)

Adoption often gets bad press, but sometimes adoption is only truly appreciated when the alternative is considered.

After I gave a talk on abortion, a lady approached me to tell the story of her friend who became pregnant as a teenager in the 1950s. Her friend decided to move away from her parents, have the baby, then put the baby up for adoption. Thirty years later she met up with her long-lost daughter. One of the first things her daughter said to her was, "Thank you, Mum, for not aborting me." She knew the alternative to adoption was death.

Let me stress at this point that abortion is not the unforgivable sin, and every man and woman reading this must know that there is no condemnation for those who are in Christ Jesus. Yet it is equally true that abortion is a tragic loss of life, when in most cases adoption is a wonderful life-affirming option.

I remember meeting an Australian Ethiopian teenager whose Australian parents adopted her. Over the years, they worked very hard to keep their daughter connected with her culture of origin. I asked this girl how she felt about being adopted. She looked me in the eye and said, "When my parents took me back to my birth parents' village, I realized the level of abject poverty and suffering I would have experienced, and I am so thankful that I am adopted".[48]

We don't always truly appreciate adoption until the alternative is considered. For those of us in Christ, the alternative to adoption is spiritual death and slavery to both sin and Satan, without any hope of eternal inheritance.

We become God's adopted children

The privilege of being led by the Spirit is that you are a son of God.[49] In Christ, we have received the Spirit of sonship. The Spirit of God functions a bit like the believer's adoption papers: the papers are signed and sealed, guaranteeing that we belong to God and that we are soon to be delivered into his loving arms on the last day.

So the call to put to death the deeds of the body happens from *inside* the family, which makes a huge difference. We don't battle with our sin in the fear of punishment. We serve the Lord without fear because, as Romans 8:1 makes clear, there is now no condemnation in Christ Jesus. Because our sin has already been condemned in the body of our Lord

---

[48] I met that girl while speaking at a church conference. She became a Christian during the week of the conference, and was even more thankful for her adoption into God's family.

[49] Don't be put off by the masculine image. Both genders have to do some cross-gender work when reading the Bible. So we men are part of the church, which is the bride of Christ, while women are to see themselves as sons of God, which, in this context, means they are full heirs of God.

Jesus, God is now our Father. The intimate prayer language of "*Abba*, Father" that marked Jesus as the eternal Son of God is now allowed to fall from our lips (cf. Mark 14:36). We are God's adopted children. While the first thing that might come to our mind when we hear the word 'Abba' is the Swedish pop band, it is actually an intimate Aramaic equivalent to the English word 'Dad'.

It was Augustine, one of the early church fathers, who first noted that by combining the Aramaic (*Abba*) and Greek (*pater*) words for 'father', Jesus' prayer pointed to the inclusion of both Jews and Gentiles into God's family. We are all one in Christ.

It may have been rare, but it wasn't new for God to be viewed as the Father of Israel (Mal 1:6). So it was not surprising that Jesus, the eternal and unique Son of God, would call his God not just 'Father' but 'Abba'. What is breathtaking is that we, who were once enemies of God, are not only forgiven but also adopted. It's one thing for the guilty to be acquitted, but it is quite another for the guilty to be adopted into God's family and given full rights as family members. Only those in Christ are given permission to call the judge of the living and the dead 'Dad'.[50] We are brought into the most intimate relationship with the Creator of the universe.

Thomas Watson captured the stunning privilege of adoption when he wrote, "If a man adopts another for his heir, he will not adopt his mortal enemy; but that God should adopt

---

50 We have allowed this privilege to be trivialized, in part by inviting unbelievers to call God by the name that should only be used by his saved, adopted children. I truly have mixed feelings when Christians want to fight for the Lord's Prayer to be prayed at the opening of parliament, when the majority or our MPs don't know Christ.

us, when we were not only strangers, but enemies, is the wonder of his love".[51]

Any conversation with an informed Muslim will tell you this notion is truly radical. Throughout the entire Qur'an, a Muslim is never permitted to address Allah in such personal terms. There may be 99 names for God in the Qur'an, but not one of them is 'Father'. In her book, *I Dared to Call Him Father*, Muslim convert Bilquis Sheikh describes her conversion and her tentative understanding that the God she now believed in was her heavenly Father:

> "O Father, my Father... Father God."
>
> Hesitantly, I spoke His name aloud. I tried different ways of speaking to Him. And then, as if something broke through for me I found myself trusting that He was indeed hearing me, just as my earthly father had always done.
>
> "Father, O my Father God", I cried, with growing confidence. My voice seemed unusually loud in the large bedroom as I knelt on the rug beside my bed. But suddenly that room wasn't empty anymore. He was there![52]

---

51 Thomas Watson, *A Body of Divinity*, Banner of Truth, London, 1958 (originally published 1692), p. 163. "Plato gave God thanks that he had made him a man, and not only a man but a philosopher; but it is infinitely more, that he should invest us with the prerogative of sons. It is love for God to feed us, but more to adopt us."

52 Bilquis Sheikh with Richard H Schneider, *I Dared To Call Him Father: The Miraculous Story of a Muslim Woman's Encounter with God*, Chosen Books, Grand Rapids, 2003, p. 48. I am indebted to Mike Raiter, who shared this quote with me.

After a lifetime of being taught that Allah was distant, removed, impersonal and unknowable, four decades of instruction was reversed in a split second when the Spirit brought her to new birth, persuading her and testifying to her that God was her Father.

As a young Christian, I still remember a friend of mine beginning his prayer, "Dear Heavenly Dad". I can tell you that I didn't like it. I think it felt a touch presumptuous and a touch, dare I say, corny. But the problem was mine, not his. He had a God-given right to approach God with such boldness. The Spirit of sonship had adopted him and given him permission to cry out "*Abba*, Father"—"Father Dad".[53]

JI Packer, one of the great theologians in recent church history, makes the insightful comment that adoption, not justification, is the highest privilege that the gospel offers:

> As justification is the *primary* blessing, so it is the *fundamental* blessing, in the sense that everything else in our salvation assumes it, and rests on it—adoption included.
>
> But this is not to say that justification is the *highest* blessing of the gospel. Adoption is higher, because

---

[53] Lloyd-Jones notes that one purpose of our adoption is to provide "great assurance when we pray and to [help us] realize that God is ready to listen to us. Think of the analogy of an earthly parent who may be very busy on some occasion. He may be a man of great affairs—the head of a great business, or a great professional man, whose program is unusually full. Someone wants to see him; but he sends out a message to say that he cannot see anyone, however important. Suddenly he hears a little tap at his door, and he knows that it is his little child or grandchild who is there; immediately he stops working and opens the door. God is like that! God is our Father, and He is ready to listen to us, and to bear with us" (The Sons of God, p. 164).

of the richer relationship with God that it involves...
Justification is a *forensic* idea, conceived in terms of *law*, and viewing God as *judge*...

Adoption is a *family* idea, conceived in terms of *love*, and viewing God as *father*. In adoption, God takes us into His family and fellowship, and establishes us as His children and heirs. Closeness, affection and generosity are at the heart of the relationship. To be right with God the judge is a great thing, but to be loved and cared for by God the father is greater.[54]

And as a good and loving father, God wants us to know we are his children. We have already been told that God has poured out his love into our hearts through the Holy Spirit (Rom 5:5). Now we see a complementary aspect of the Holy Spirit's ministry, one of the most wonderful ministries of the Spirit: to assure and convince the believer that they belong to God—"The Spirit himself testifies with our spirit that we are God's children" (8:16).

Notice that it's in the context of praying to God as our Father (8:15) that his Spirit confirms to us that we are God's children. That is why I suspect that to pray "in the Spirit" is to pray to God as 'Father' (cf. Eph 2:18, 6:18). This might also explain the fact that when we stop praying for long periods of time, we often lack the experience of assurance that comes with prayer. We grumble at not feeling God's presence, and yet we refuse to give expression to our relationship with our heavenly Father by calling out to him. Our union with Christ is not destroyed by a lack of prayer, but our experience of the

---

[54] JI Packer, *Knowing God*, Hodder & Stoughton, London, 1973, pp. 186-8.

joy of that union certainly suffers whenever we fail to speak to our heavenly Father.

One Christian counsellor I know required all her new Christian clients to commit to spending 20 minutes each day talking to their heavenly Father about the issue they were concerned about, before they met with her for their first session. She reported that more than a few said they didn't need to come. Drawing near to their Father in heaven was exactly what they needed to do.

The promise is that God bears witness to our spirit that we are children of God. However, he doesn't bear witness to me about you. I cannot have the same level of certainty about another's salvation that I have about my own. It is not unknown for a person to marry someone in good faith—someone they reasonably thought was a genuine Christian—only to find two months, two years, or 15 years later that their partner has walked away from Christ. God does not promise that everyone who appears to be a genuine believer will prove to have had a genuine faith. And yet this wonderful promise from God remains: his Spirit, who has been poured into our hearts, testifies to each and every believer that he or she is, indeed, a child of God.

We become co-heirs with Christ

As sons of God, everything that belongs to Christ now belongs to us, his adopted children: "Now if we are children, then we are heirs—heirs of God and co-heirs with Christ, if indeed we share in his sufferings in order that we may also share in his glory" (Rom 8:17).

Look at the extravagance of all that is ours: with Christ as our older brother, we share in his glory and in his authority. We are in the will, with a guaranteed inheritance. This fits with what Paul says later in Romans 8, when he notes that "He who did not spare his own Son but gave him up for us all—how will he not also, along with him, graciously give us all things?" (v. 32).

The provision of Christ on the cross is certainly the costliest gift God will ever give to his people, but it certainly will not be the only gift. The benefits of Jesus' death and resurrection make up the "all things" referred to in verse 32. They include our election, our forgiveness, our redemption, our adoption, our place in the new creation, our glorified bodies, and of course the joy of seeing God face-to-face. When it comes to God, we're not just inheriting a few tatty old family heirlooms that no-one else wanted. We're getting the lot.

One Christmas Eve, a former Australian governor-general invited a number of homeless teenagers to come and enjoy his residence. The street kids were polite, amazed, and very appreciative. One boy was interviewed for the TV news, and he talked with wonder about how the Governor-General's residence was so big and beautiful, and about his awe when he tasted the food prepared by a professional chef. The boy loved the pool, and was particularly honoured that the Governor-General even lent his own swimming trunks to the boy. At this point the interviewer asked the boy, "Could you want for anything more?" As quick as a flash the boy responded, "Yes. I wish he would adopt me."

It's one thing to taste the life of the privileged few for a couple of hours (some might even call it a little cruel). But adoption means it's *all yours, for all time.* The homeless teenager knew exactly what he was saying when he answered the journalist's question. Our adoption as God's children means that *all* of God's blessings are *all ours, for all time.*

We will live with God in glory

As adopted children of God, not only do we have an intimate 'Dad' relationship with him, and not only do we become heirs of all that is his. We will also get to live with God forever.

For a time, my wife Sandy worked as a teacher in the same school that our children attended. During class, all the students referred to her as Mrs Galea, but at the end of the day only the Galea children were allowed to call her 'Mum', and only the Galea children went home with her.

Only those in Christ are sons of God and have the Spirit. They alone have the privilege of calling God 'Father', and only they will get to go home with the Lord Jesus.

Where to now with my anger?

My vulnerability to sinning in anger means I have be on guard with this struggle. It's a day-by-day battle. Here are some of the things I do.

1. I have to watch my diary and not overbook myself. (When I get too busy, my fuse gets shorter.) So much of godliness is prevention.
2. I have put in my daily electronic diary reminder the phrase, "Today don't be grumpy".

3. I've asked one of my fellow pastors to pray for me at the beginning of each Sunday, asking God to help me manage whatever stress happens that day with Christlike patience.
4. I dedicate a section of my prayer cards to the topic of anger. For example, I've written down the following sentences to read in my prayer time. It's a combination of simple self-talk and asking God to change me by his Spirit:

- I have never won by losing my temper.
- I have always, always, always regretted losing my temper.
- It never does any good.
- It grieves God's Spirit, who guarantees the redemption of my body.
- It grieves the people that I dump on, such as my wife, my children, and others.

5. When I fail, I rush to the cross and know that our Lord sits on a throne of grace to help me in my time of need (Heb 4:16). In Christ, I can't make God angry!

I am first and foremost a child of God, not an angry man.

The good news is that, by God's grace, I'm making progress. Charlotte, my daughter-in-law of six years, said recently that she has never seen me lose my temper—praise the Lord! (I wish the staff at my church could say the same.) God is doing what he promised: he is transforming me from one degree of glory to the next.

So I join with many other sulking, sarcastic, intimidating anger addicts, and I say with John Newton (author of 'Amazing Grace'):

Yet though I am not what I ought to be, nor what I wish to be, nor what I hope to be, I can truly say I am not what I once was—a slave to sin and Satan; and I can heartily join with the Apostle, and acknowledge, "By the grace of God I am what I am".[55]

Come Lord Jesus!

55 Quoted in *The Christian Pioneer*, vol. 10, no. 115, January 1856, p. 84.

Intermission

Now, as we come to the end of section one of this book, let's ask some hard and personal questions.

- Is the Christian life liveable? Yes!
- Will you achieve sinlessness in this life? No!
- Will you ever be tempted beyond what you are able to bear? Not according to our Lord![56]
- Will you be forgiven again and again, even if you fall many times? Absolutely!
- Can you confess your sin privately to God and not tell anyone? Not if you want real change.
- Are you strong enough on your own to change? No way!
- Is the Spirit in you powerful enough to transform you? Definitely!

---

56 This is not a promise of sinless perfectionism. It is, amongst other things, recognition that I am always responsible for whatever sin I commit. There is never a sin for which I don't have to say sorry to God and to others. But because God's Spirit is at work in me to change me, I *can* resist any temptation. I always have a fighting chance.

Do you hate how recurring sin is destroying your life and grieving God's Spirit? Is it bad enough yet? Have you hit rock bottom?

You know that whatever comfort your sin gives you, whatever false intimacy you've enjoyed, whatever heightened experience you get, no matter how alive you may feel in the moment, the moment it's over you feel dead. All you have is an awful, empty, lonely, shameful, withdrawn, hypocritical, numbing feeling.

What do you do when you reach that point? It's critical that you run into the arms of your Father in heaven. If you don't, there is only one place left to run: back to the sin, if for no other reason than to relieve yourself of the burden of guilt. We must let Jesus, through his Spirit, take us to the Father, who is seated on a throne of grace and who sets us free for his glory. In other words, take up the call to put sin to death within the family. And as you (and the Spirit) put your sin to death, experience the deep sense of joy that lasts right through into eternity.

So the first section of this book gives us the framework in which God's children engage in the battle with sin and the sinful nature. In summary, Romans 8:1-17 speaks of what it means to be "in the flesh": left to our natural state (in Adam) we would remain hostile to God, not only unwilling but also unable to submit to him, let alone please him.

But God did what his law could not do by sending his Son to be a sin offering. Not only is there now no condemnation for those who are "'in Christ Jesus", but by his Spirit we have received both "life" and "peace". The Spirit has made our body his home and has also made us alive, creating newfound desires to do God's will by enabling us to say 'no' to sin.

The Spirit will one day raise our mortal bodies to life, just as he raised Christ. The indwelling Spirit is also our 'adoption paper', testifying that we are his children and guaranteeing our future inheritance. As sons of God, all that belongs to Christ now belongs to us in Christ. And best of all, the God and judge of the universe is our Dad. This is revolutionary! We undertake the battle with sin *within* the family of God, where there is absolutely no condemnation in Christ Jesus.

Why not take some time now to praise God for the many blessings you have received?

Dear God,
You are the Father I never had, your Son the Lord Jesus is the brother I wish I'd had, and you have given me your Spirit, whom I desperately need to live for your pleasure. Thank you for forgiving me for my daily failures, and thank you for making the changes in my life that I could never make, for apart from you Lord, I can do nothing!
In Jesus' name,
Amen

Part II
LIVING WITH SUFFERING
ROMANS 8:17-39

*I*f you do not have a robust understanding of suffering through God's eyes, you will not survive well in the Christian life. Your suffering, or the suffering of others, will hijack or harm your faith. Maybe you'll end up like Bob Hawke, former Prime Minister of Australia, who was once a professing Christian but became an agnostic after seeing enormous levels of poverty in India.

The biographer of Steve Jobs, former CEO of Apple, recounts this story:

> Even though they were not fervent about their faith, Jobs' parents wanted him to have a religious upbringing, so they took him to the Lutheran church most Sundays. That came to an end when he was thirteen. In July 1968 *Life* magazine published a shocking cover showing a pair of starving children in Biafra. Jobs took it to Sunday school and confronted the church's pastor.
>
> "If I raise my finger, will God know which one I'm going to raise even before I do it?"
>
> The pastor answered, "Yes, God knows everything".
>
> Jobs then pulled out the *Life* cover and asked, "Well, does God know about this and what's going to happen to those children?"
>
> "Steve, I know you don't understand, but yes, God knows about that."
>
> Jobs announced that he didn't want to have anything to do with worshipping such a God, and he never went back to church. He did, however, spend years studying and trying to practice the tenets of Zen Buddhism.[57]

---

57 Walter Isaacson, *Steve Jobs*, Simon & Schuster, New York, 2011, pp. 14-15.

The tragedy is that Steve Jobs rejected Christianity based on one brief discussion on suffering that he had as a teenager, yet he was prepared to spend years studying Zen Buddhism—a philosophy that denies the very existence of evil and suffering.[58] It appears that he never explored what the Bible had to say on this key issue. Had he done so, he would have found that the answers, while not complete, are profoundly more satisfying than any other worldview.

Most tragically of all, Steve Jobs never grasped the life-changing reality that God himself came to this earth knowing that he would be a sin offering, knowing that he would endure pain. God chose to enter our suffering and bear our shame and pain—but he did so in order to usher in a new universe, where children will never need to starve again.

When you consider Steve Jobs' objection to the God of the Bible, it's a touch ironic that in recent years so many millions of Africans have come to Christ, realizing that the ultimate solution to poverty—both physical and spiritual—is found through Christ bringing in a new creation.[59]

---

58 See Keith Yandell and Harold Netland, *Buddhism: A Christian Exploration and Appraisal*, IVP Academic, Downers Grove, 2009. The authors reflect on how a consistent Zen Buddhist would approach the Holocaust. They note that "From the perspective of ultimate reality, emptiness, we cannot condemn the Holocaust as evil since moral categories do not apply on that level" (p. 102).
59 "In 1900, Christians comprised 9 per cent of the African population and were outnumbered by Muslims four to one. Today, Christians comprise 44 per cent of the population, and in the 1960s passed Muslims in number" (Keller, *The Reason for God*, p. 41).

Our battle against suffering

If the first part of Romans 8 deals with the power of the Spirit to enable us to engage in the battle against sin and the sinful nature, then the second part deals with our battle against suffering. Our suffering can often make us introspective, resentful and bitter, but Paul locates our suffering on a much larger canvas. In the process, he helps us make some sense of our angst.

Before we start looking at Romans 8:17-39, we need to acknowledge one important question that is not answered for us in the Bible: why is suffering unevenly distributed among humans, and among Christians? To my mind, this is a mystery that has no revealed answer in the Scriptures.

Some seem to live life on a bed of roses and then die in their sleep at 95 years of age. Others come into this world from the womb of a 15-year-old mother who is addicted to ice, while never knowing their father. The same person may endure a loveless marriage that results in three children (one with Down Syndrome) and five miscarriages, before being diagnosed with inoperable cancer at the age of 48.

It's not that the first person did not experience any suffering—there are always thorns among the roses—but objectively speaking it can't compare with the second story.

Suffering is unevenly distributed. When we look for nice neat explanations, as Job's three friends did (that's the Job in the Bible, not Steve), wrong solutions inevitably follow. It's obvious that some suffering is brought on directly by our stupid behaviour—such as getting drunk, driving a car into a tree, and ending up with a crushed spine. And yet we know of many people who drive over the prescribed alcohol limits but are kept from serious consequences. Why one and not the other? No direct answer is given.

What we do know is that all suffering is experienced by people who live outside the garden of Eden and after the fall of Adam, which means God is not unjust in his dealings with his fallen image-bearers. We must never forget that, left to ourselves, we are by nature objects of God's wrath (Eph 2:3). This is a basic tenet of Scripture. Lose this framework, and our focus will be on the disparity of suffering. This often leads to self-pity, rather than the joy that can be ours in Christ even in the midst of suffering: the joy that looks forward to the glory that lies before us. It will be worth it!

In the meantime, we weep with those who weep, and we mourn with those who mourn (Rom 12:15).

7

Now you cry "Why?", but then...
Romans 8:17-18

¹⁷ Now if we are children, then we are heirs—heirs of God and co-heirs with Christ, if indeed we share in his sufferings in order that we may also share in his glory.

¹⁸ I consider that our present sufferings are not worth comparing with the glory that will be revealed in us. (Rom 8:17-18)

I remember vividly the day a woman in our church told me that she had a cancerous tumour the size of a tennis ball in her uterus. She knew it was serious when the doctor delayed his holiday by one day to see her for further tests. There was a good chance that she could die.

She had two boys, both under five, and she was a single parent. I reflected back to her that she seemed to be handling the news very well. She said, "Yes, both the doctor and my parents have noticed my calmness. I'm just waiting for them to ask me why I am so calm." Then she added, "It's so unlike me, Ray. I'm normally the one who feels sorry for myself because of all the things that have happened to me." It wasn't that she was unconcerned for her children. But she was able to face the possibility of her own death with a degree of expectant joy at the glory that awaited her. Her suffering made her hungry for heaven.

This woman was letting suffering do the work God intends it to do. Paul has already written about one of the purposes of suffering in Romans 5: "And we boast in the hope of the glory of God. Not only so, but we also glory in our sufferings, because we know that suffering produces perseverance; perseverance, character; and character, hope" (Rom 5:2-4).

Suffering can stimulate hope, as it unbolts the door of the heart and allows the promises of God, which are so easily spoken but sometimes go unheard, to find their mark and actually be believed.

The suffering on view in Romans 8 includes all that this broken world has to offer. Later in this chapter, in verse 35, Paul lists several types of suffering—most of which he would have experienced firsthand. These include *trouble, hardship, persecution, famine, nakedness, danger* and *sword*. Clearly, there is no prosperity gospel in this age—not for this apostle, or for anyone else.

Our sufferings can't compare with our future glory

How does God expect us to cope with our quota of suffering? It is by understanding the big picture and living in light of the end: "I consider that our present sufferings are not worth comparing with the glory that will be revealed in us" (8:18).

When you measure the suffering now with the glory to come, it just doesn't compare. When Paul says he 'considers', he is using the word to describe the thinking of an accountant when he lines up the credit and the debit. The cost of a $2 ticket can't compete with the windfall of a three-million-dollar lottery win. They just don't compare. It's as calculated as that.

Now you ask, "Why, Lord?" Then, in glory, you will say, "It was so worth it!"

I came to a fresh appreciation of this principle several years ago. To understand the story I'm about to share, you need to enter into the mind of a sports fan. We are doggedly loyal to whichever team we follow. It's part of our DNA. And yes, I know it's irrational and profoundly superficial. But the emotional life of a sports fan rides on the back of our team's success or failure.

In my case, I am a St George Illawarra Dragons rugby league tragic. We had not won a grand final in 30 years, even though we played in five grand finals during that time. I was there for the fifth loss in 1999, and, even though we were ahead 14-0 at half time, we still managed to lose. It was devastating.

Then in 2009, a new coach arrived: the venerable Wayne Bennett. Just over a year later, on October 3rd 2010, I was at the ground watching the mighty Dragons win their first grand final in over three decades. We won by 32 points to 8 over the Roosters, the same team that defeated us in the 1975 grand final by 38-0. This made the win that much sweeter.

The winning feeling was simply euphoric. After the game

we went to the Dragons' home ground with thousands of other red and white fans, walking on the hallowed ground of Jubilee Oval, hugging and high-fiving strangers. It was a surreal moment. We then collectively walked to the St George Leagues Club, but not before stopping the traffic as we danced in the streets.

Here's the point: through the whole experience, I kept thinking to myself that the joy of this grand final win was worth all the disappointment over the past three decades. Indeed, remembering those past frustrations now served to enhance the glory of this moment.

During the celebrations, I remembered Romans 8:18. I imagined myself with others in the new creation, looking back on all our suffering in this world and saying, "It was so worth it! Our past sufferings can't compare to the glory that we're experiencing now." It's not that we won't remember the pain. It's just that it won't compare with the inexpressible joy of the age to come.

At this point, we must understand that suffering is not optional for the Christian. The Messiah's people cannot expect to walk down a road that is different from their crucified, suffering Messiah: "Now if we are children of God, then we are heirs—heirs of God and co-heirs with Christ, *if indeed* we share in his sufferings in order that we may also share in his glory" (8:17). We cannot escape the fact that this is a conditional statement. No suffering means no glory! It is God's expectation that, in this age, Christians will share in the suffering of their Lord.

Some of this suffering will come from persecution as a result of our loyalty to our Saviour. Perhaps the least loved promise of God is that "everyone who wants to live a godly life in Christ Jesus will be persecuted" (2 Tim 3:12). A godly Christian life leads to persecution—not only for some, but for all. Our union with Christ includes the fact that we have been crucified, we have died, we've been buried, and we've been raised with Christ as co-heirs with him in the heavenly realms. However, our union with Christ also extends to the fact that we will share in his sufferings. As John Stott puts it, "So the sufferings and the glory are married; they cannot be divorced. They are welded; they cannot be broken apart."[60]

The promise of heaven on earth is not the Bible's promise. We live with mortal bodies that will one day be resurrected. We live with mortal bodies in a mortal world that has a use-by date. For now, it is God's expectation that suffering is part of the life of the Christian.

So the question about suffering in your life is not a question of 'if' but 'when'. For many, it's truly a present reality. As I write these words my church is covering in prayer a 14-year-old boy named Jake, who is dearly loved but who has serious spinal injuries, the outcome of which is as yet uncertain. No doubt you can easily think of many who are facing the present sufferings that are part and parcel of life in this broken world.

Because suffering is inevitable, it is critical that you get your thinking straight (as best you can) *before* you enter into the experience of suffering. Verses 17 and 18 don't contain the only things to be said on suffering, nor do they stop the pain and tears and doubts, but they are critical in helping us to be ready when the suffering comes.

When I was a boy, the ads on TV for the latest toy promised

---

60 Stott, *The Message of Romans*, p. 237.

so much, but the reality always left you disappointed. Those toys over-promised and under-delivered. The racing cars wouldn't stay on the track, the batteries were not supplied, and the controls were faulty. There was a recurring sense of disappointment.

It won't be like that when we finally enter into the presence of God. You won't be feeling sorry for yourself because of your sufferings on earth. As you step into the new creation you won't be saying, "Gee, I thought it would be better than this". You won't even know the meaning of the word 'disappointment'. It will truly be perfect one day, perfect the next.

So, as you take your place in the new creation, no doubt you will bump into the Russian Christian who was incarcerated for eight years in a Siberian prison because of his faith in Christ. Or the Canadian woman who lived with a broken back after a diving accident on a Christian camp. Or perhaps the young Jewish man whose father disinherited him because he professed faith in Jesus the Messiah. Or the Chinese mother who witnessed the death of her two children in a car accident where she was the driver.

Now picture yourself in the new creation saying to them, "I'm so sorry to hear of your pain back in the old creation", and "My, didn't you receive a horrific quota of suffering!" Have no doubt that they will turn to you and, with a bemused expression, look you in the eye and say, "Suffering? What suffering? I barely know what you're talking about. But isn't it just so awesome to be here in the presence of God and to share in his glory!"

"I consider that our present sufferings are not worth comparing with the glory that will be revealed in us" (8:18).

Clinging to the promise of future glory
Paul Grimmond

My own experience of suffering has been largely internal rather than external. I have struggled on and off in my life with anxiety and depression. I am a pastor, and in my late 20s I was handed the role of senior pastor in a large ministry with only two years of experience post-Bible college. In the first year of that ministry, my father-in-law slowly wasted away and then went home to Jesus because of a brain tumour.

Over the following years, as I tried desperately to keep up with the responsibilities of the job (budgets, staffing, preaching multiple times a week) and of being a husband and father with three small children, I found my body and my mind slowly giving up. I would find myself listening to pastoral problems and realizing that I didn't care. On occasions I preached God's word and then came down from the pulpit feeling nothing at all. I felt deeply unclean. I felt my stomach clenching in dread as I looked in my diary and saw the next parish council meeting coming.

By the time I had been in the job for five years, I found myself curled up in a ball on the bedroom floor, feeling totally defeated and almost unable to move. In God's kindness, I started to work out that I needed to leave the job, but that just multiplied the guilt. I remember that as my time leading that church came to an end, I addressed a pastor's conference about my situation and left the podium in tears, exclaiming what I felt: "I am a complete failure. I feel like a complete failure."

So what can I say about God's precious promise that our

present sufferings are not worth comparing with the glory to be revealed in us? Even at the time, these words were precious. But I also struggled to feel them and completely trust the truth of them. I believed that they were true intellectually; I just found it hard to *feel* their truth. In God's kindness, however, I can now (eight years later) say a little more.

Firstly, I can now see enough of what God has done, even in this life, to know that what God gives in suffering is more valuable than what he takes. I look back now and am able to say, "I would go through that again". Not that everything is perfect—I still have days when I struggle. And I certainly don't ever want to experience the darkness that I felt back then, if God will spare me. But I am thankful to God for his kindness in using that time in my life to bring growth and trust that I would never have had without it. I have come to understand myself better (and repent of some of my sinful people-centredness). I have learned more about how to love my wife, and our marriage has grown as a result. And God has shown me more clearly that he is deeply trustworthy.

How much more wonderful, then, is the promise that God will one day grant to us such a weight of glory that our present sufferings will look as nothing. What a joy that day will be. Praise be to God!

8

Groaning for glory
Romans 8:19-22

¹⁹ For the creation waits in eager expectation for the children of God to be revealed. ²⁰ For the creation was subjected to frustration, not by its own choice, but by the will of the one who subjected it, in hope ²¹ that the creation itself will be liberated from its bondage to decay and brought into the freedom and glory of the children of God.

²² We know that the whole creation has been groaning as in the pains of childbirth right up to the present time. (Rom 8:19-22)

*I*t's hard to wait.

When my kids were younger, we would often travel for five hours to the NSW north coast for our summer holidays. As the journey dragged on, one of them would inevitably cry out in an exasperated tone: "WHEN. ARE. WE. GOING. TO. GET. THERE??" I distinctly remember each word being emphasized for dramatic effect.

We are able to persevere as we share in the sufferings of Christ only because we confidently look forward to sharing in his glory in the age to come. The idea of waiting 'eagerly', with 'eager longing' and with 'patience', comes up three times in this section of Romans (8:19, 23, 25). And you don't eagerly await a possibility. We are, so to speak, bursting with hopeful certainty as we wait with confidence for the glory that is coming. There is no notion of 'fingers crossed'—that is for those who believe in fate. God is not cruel, and he takes no delight in leaving you with doubt. It is the glory that *will* be revealed in us. When this glory is revealed, we won't be watching from a distance on the sideline (as I was with my team's grand final win). The glory is revealed or unveiled *in us*. It will involve our whole being, body and soul.

But that is then. And this is now. In this age, we are left to groan. Sitting through a long car trip is one thing, but enduring the sufferings of life in this broken world is something else again.

It's hard to wait.

The word 'groaning' is used three times in Romans 8 (vv. 22, 23, 26). It describes not so much what some tennis players do when they serve, but what your mother was doing when she gave birth to you. I'm told that for first-time mothers, the average time for active labour is 14 long hours. No matter how long it took for your mother, you can be sure she wasn't singing a few bars of 'What a Wonderful World' as she gave birth to you. She was groaning.

Who exactly is doing the groaning here in Romans? In the three verses where the word is used, three very different identities are described as groaning: the whole creation

(v. 22), Christians (v. 23), and the Spirit himself (v. 26). We'll look at the groaning of creation in this chapter, and the groanings of the Christian and of the Spirit in the next chapter.

Creation groans, awaiting its liberation

First, we see that the creation itself groans, reminding us that this is a world awaiting its liberation. We will start with verse 22 and track backwards:

> We know that the whole creation has been groaning as in the pains of children birth right up to the present time. (v. 22)

By 'creation', Paul is referring to the totality of the universe. Paul personifies creation with its groaning, but not because it is actually a 'person', like 'Mother Nature'. Paul personifies the non-personal universe to make a powerful point: creation is groaning, and has been groaning since sin entered the world, right up to the present time—and not simply some sections of it, but all of it. It's not just creation in the 21st century where massive tankers spew oil onto precious coral reefs, or where climate change seems to pose significant threats to our future. Creation also groans in the untouched portions of a Tasmanian forest, just as it does on the back of an industrial spillage.

The suffering of God's people, which is Paul's focus, is viewed here within the much bigger picture of the whole of creation. Just as Israel groaned under slavery in Egypt while looking for freedom (cf. Exod 3:7), so creation itself is looking for its own liberating exodus: "The creation itself will be liberated from its bondage to decay and brought into the freedom and glory of the children of God" (Rom 8:21).

The natural world, though reflecting and declaring the glory of its Creator (cf. Ps 19:1-6; Rom 1:19-20), is in bondage to decay. The language of decay "seems to denote not only that the universe is running down (as we would say), but that nature is also enslaved, locked into an unending cycle, so that conception, birth and growth are relentlessly followed by decline, decay, death and decomposition".[61] Creation has failed to realize its potential, for it is a fallen world.

One of the pictures of a new creation ushered in by the Spirit-filled Messiah is of cosmic reconciliation, where "The wolf will live with the lamb, the leopard will lie down with the goat" (Isa 11:6). My sister used to have a sticker on her wardrobe mirror with a picture of a lamb and a lion lying down together, along with the words 'Coming Soon'. In this age, you put a wolf and lamb together and an hour later there is just a wolf licking its lips. It's hard to grasp an alternate creation, when we have no other experience than that of living in a fallen world.

Like humans who bear God's image and yet are fallen and enslaved to the fear of death, so creation can reveal the glory of God in its beauty and majesty, yet still be subjected to frustration. Just as Francis Schaeffer would refer to humanity as a glorious ruin, so it would be correct to describe creation

---

61 Stott, *The Message of Romans*, p. 239.

itself in the same way; part glory and part ruin.[62]

But the present state of creation was not God's ultimate goal. Paul speaks with a ring of confidence when he says that the creation will achieve its God-given destiny, where it will finally be liberated from its bondage to decay: "For the creation was subjected to frustration, not by its own choice, but by the will of the one who subjected it…" (Rom 8:20).

Notice that it was God—not humans, and not Satan—who subjected creation to its bondage to decay. Paul may well be referring to Genesis 3:17-19, where the created order is cursed because of Adam's sin. It was not only Eve and her descendants who would experience the pain of childbirth; the whole of creation has experienced God's curse ever since. But here we are not simply talking about the fact that carbon dioxide concentrations have increased by 40 per cent since pre-industrial times, resulting in significant climate change. We are talking about the very structure and nature of creation itself, which is in bondage to decay due to God's decree as a result of the sin of the first man. It appears that the natural world has always paid the price for foolish, sinful humans.

It is not uncommon to be told that the natural world is a perfectly balanced ecosystem that would thrive in its own pristine natural condition, if only we humans would get out of its way. But from God's vantage point, this creation is groaning, and this side of the new heavens and the new earth it always will be. The best is yet to come—not just for God's

---

62 Francis Schaeffer, 'Part 17—The Fall', lecture given on 1 January 1980, Biblical Doctrine Series: Westminster Confession, *L'Abri Ideas Library*, available online (viewed 18 April 2017): www.labri-ideas-library.org/download.asp?fileID=116.

people but for the whole of God's creation.[63] It was God who brought the creation to its enslavement, and it is God who will set it free. When God cursed the ground, it was only temporarily, in the hope of ultimate cosmic redemption.

Our liberation and creation's liberation are linked

Creation's ticket to freedom rides on the back of the liberation of God's people:

> The creation waits in eager expectation for the children of God to be revealed. (Rom 8:19)

The resurrection of God's children will spearhead the arrival of the new heavens and new earth. What God had intended for his world right back "in the beginning" (Genesis 1) will finally come to fruition.

Without in any way denying our responsibility to be good stewards of our current environment, Christians are the ultimate greenies. This is because creation eagerly awaits its liberation on the day of the Lord, when the children of God will be liberated and glorified. One liberation will trigger the other.

It is God's commitment to the natural world that obligates us to share in that commitment, in the same way that God's

---

[63] Perhaps the Law of Increasing Entropy has always been making this point. Age, disease and the death of all living things are tied directly to the Second Law of Thermodynamics (sometimes referred to as the Law of Increasing Entropy).

commitment to the resurrection of the body requires us to be good stewards of our bodies. It would badly miss the point if the truth that creation awaits divine liberation causes us to abandon our responsibility to care for creation. God has entrusted to us humans, made in his image, the responsibility to rule and care for this world (Gen 1:28, 2:15). We ought to take care of this earth as people entrusted with a precious gift, and as stewards who will have to give an account to the Creator. Not only that, we must take care of it because we don't know when our Lord Jesus will return, and our love for others demands that we pass this earth to the next generation in better condition than when we received it.

And yet our framework for ecology must include a biblical understanding that creation is, indeed, subject to futility by its bondage to decay. Human effort will never restore the earth to pristine condition. Its freedom will only come when Jesus returns and the saints are set free. The focus remains on Christ, and on us being in Christ. Any other approach to ecology moves in the direction of idolatry.

At the risk of overstatement, there are three conversions awaiting every person. The first and most critical conversion results in a new and wonderful personal relationship with Jesus, resulting in a shift from death to life, from slave to free, from enemy to friend. The second 'conversion' involves grasping the place of the church in God's design. God is saving for himself a people, not just individuals. You cannot love Jesus unless you love his people. The third 'conversion' is to grasp the cosmic nature of our salvation. Coming to Christ means I am forgiven, and it means I am part of God's people—but it also means the creation of a glorious new heavens and a new earth, which will no longer groan in its frustration to death and decay. All of which inspires us to preach the gospel of our Lord Jesus Christ.

Paul has shown us that suffering is inevitable in the Christian life. Part of that suffering happens because we live in a creation that is groaning, subject to frustration. But that suffering will come to an end. This is the point that Paul takes up in the next part of Romans 8.

Trusting God's unfailing love
Julie Lamplough

Nearly five years ago, I was diagnosed with early breast cancer. My diagnosis was followed by lots of weeping and crying. My youngest was only 16 months old, and I cried uncontrollably as I hugged my three children, thinking my death was imminent.

You could imagine my joy when my oncologist told me I was curable—although I was stunned at first, as I had warned everybody I was going to die. I did everything my doctors told me to do to make my cure a reality: surgery (which disfigured my body), chemotherapy (which stole my hair), and radiation (which burned me and tightened the muscles that it hit). Throughout it all I trusted in God, especially when most of my treatment produced only minimal side effects. I sensed God's presence and completely trusted him. I pictured him holding me in his arms like a parent would hold a child. I thought I was on the home stretch when, two years after my initial diagnosis, I was given the 'all clear'. Six months later I underwent reconstructive surgery. I thought God was slowly restoring my body and I was excited about what lay ahead. I looked and felt good.

However, four weeks after my surgery, some unexpected pain in my right shoulder led to a CT scan, where the doctors were looking for lung clots. Instead, they found that my cancer had returned with a vengeance. It had spread to my bones and to the lymph nodes in my chest. This time, I was told the cancer was inoperable and incurable.

I was shattered.

I did everything I could to minimise the cancer's effect on my body. The latest treatments offered the possibility of years of extended life. After an amazing prayer meeting with my church and my family, I felt emboldened to fight this disease. I researched and read ahead, much to the annoyance of my oncologist at the time. Unfortunately the treatments either did not work for me, or they didn't work for very long. I paid thousands of dollars for the final treatment, and I convinced myself it was the only chance for my cancer to shrink away. My new oncologist was in favour of it. However, it did anything but what it was supposed to do. It made my cancer surge ahead and put me closer to the end of my life.

To be honest, I felt very angry and disappointed with God—but I know I didn't have any right to be. He is the author and sustainer of life; he has the right to take it away. And, amid the failed treatments, he has given me two years of life when I should have died long ago. I remember reading through the book of Job, expecting to find that my negative feelings towards God were justified. Instead, I felt even more convicted of my sin and self-righteousness. I submitted to

God's will and authority over me, even if it meant death, and I chose to trust in his unfailing love.

I prepare more for the worst these days. I know that this world is due to expire. I think about heaven, and about the reality that there will be no more crying or pain. This suffering that I'm enduring is only for now. Compared to eternity, it is short-lived. In eternity, God will completely restore me and make me strong, firm and steadfast. Waiting for this is hard, but I know that one day all of creation—including my body—will be "liberated from its bondage to decay".

God is the one who will look after my family when I am gone. But I still pray for mercy—that he will extend my life and allow me to see my children grow up.

9

We groan, and the Spirit groans for us
Romans 8:23-27

²³ Not only so, but **we ourselves, who have the firstfruits of the Spirit, groan** inwardly as we wait eagerly for our adoption to sonship, the redemption of our bodies. ²⁴ For in this hope we were saved. But hope that is seen is no hope at all. Who hopes for what they already have? ²⁵ But if we hope for what we do not yet have, we wait for it patiently.

²⁶ In the same way, the Spirit helps us in our weakness. We do not know what we ought to pray for, but the **Spirit himself intercedes for us through wordless groans**. ²⁷ And he who searches our hearts knows the mind of the Spirit, because the Spirit intercedes for God's people in accordance with the will of God. (Rom 8:23-27)

*A*bout 15 years ago, I decided to survey my congregation to ascertain what they really believed on a range of doctrines (as opposed to what I thought they believed). My survey contained three questions that related to the Holy Spirit. Mindful that we have non-Christians who attend each Sunday, it was pleasing to see that 92% of people agreed that the Holy Spirit is God, since he is clearly referred to as God in the Bible.[64]

However, there was some confusion as to whether or not the Holy Spirit is a person.

When asked the question "Is the Holy Spirit a force?", 21% of people agreed, while another 12% said they were not sure, and 16% did not respond. Clearly, *Star Wars* was affecting this discussion.

There is no doubt that the Holy Spirit is powerful, and in that sense he could possibly be described as a 'force' that prevails. But he is much more than just an impersonal power; he is not just like an electric current. What did people mean when they described the Holy Spirit as a force?

My fears were realized by the answers to the next question: "Is the Holy Spirit a person?" Less than half the people in my church agreed with this statement, while 38% disagreed, 2% said they were not sure, and 11% gave no answer.

It's hard to express how devastated this pastor felt knowing that, under my watch, only half of my congregation understood that the Holy Spirit is a 'he', not an 'it'.

The Spirit of God is not merely an extension of the Father or the Son; he is a distinct person in his own right. When Jesus commissions the first band of disciples to "go and make

---

64 For example, see Peter's remarks to Ananias in Acts 5:3-4.

disciples of all nations, baptizing them in the name of the Father and of the Son and of the Holy Spirit", the Spirit is every bit as much a distinct person as the Father and the Son (Matt 28:19).[65]

I took some comfort in discovering that part of the problem lay with confusion between the notion of 'person' and the idea of being 'human'. Nevertheless, the congregation was bombarded thereafter with a constant diet of teaching on the personhood of the Spirit of God.

There are numerous reasons why this matters, but in the context of Romans 8 we need to know not just *what* but *who* will help us in the face of our suffering. It is not only creation that groans like a mother in childbirth; even the sons of God themselves groan. But we don't groan alone. The *person* of the Holy Spirit comes to our aid.

---

65   In John 14-16, Jesus describes the Holy Spirit as a being who is distinct from Jesus and from the Father. Just as Jesus has the personal qualities of an advocate or a counsellor who comforts his disciples, so the Holy Spirit would be "another advocate" or "another counsellor" (John 14:16).

In the Greek language, the word for 'Spirit' has a neuter gender. Therefore, grammatically you would expect the word 'Spirit' to be referred to as an 'it'. However, in John 16:13 Jesus uses the masculine pronoun to refer to the "Spirit of truth", showing that the Holy Spirit is not an 'it' but a 'him'. The Spirit does what you would expect only a person to do: he teaches (John 14:26), he speaks and invites (Rev 22:17), he convicts (John 16:8), he intercedes for us (Rom 8:26), he is grieved (Eph 4:30; cf. Isa 63:10), and he distributes gifts as he determines (1 Cor 12:11). So as the Nicene Creed has summarized for us:

> We believe in the Holy Spirit, the Lord, the giver of life,
> who proceeds from the Father and the Son.
> With the Father and the Son he is worshipped and glorified.
> He has spoken through the prophets.

We groan awaiting our redemption

> Not only so, but we ourselves, who have the firstfruits of the Spirit, groan inwardly as we wait eagerly for our adoption to sonship, the redemption of our bodies. (Rom 8:23)

Having the Spirit does not mean we have arrived in the age to come. The future has indeed broken into the present, but not fully. Having the Spirit gives you a righteous appetite for more because we have the firstfruits—but only the firstfruits. The gift of the Spirit does not give us endless victories over suffering and sickness. Spirit-filled we may be, but we still operate within mortal bodies as part of a creation that aches. Ironically, having the Spirit makes us discontent, hungry for more, because we only have the down payment, the barest taste of the glories to come.

The language of 'firstfruits' carries the promise of more. As a farmer's reluctant son, I remember growing up knowing that if the first pick of the crops was good, then it guaranteed that more was to follow. (This would please my dad no end, but not me—as a kid all I could think about was that it just meant more work!) The firstfruits of the Spirit are the down payment guaranteeing that the rest will follow. The best is yet to come!

The 'more to come' is our adoption, which will include the complete restoration of our bodies. Notice that it's not redemption *from* our bodies. Our final goal is not to end up looking like Casper the Friendly Ghost. The language of redemption and adoption intersect at this point. Redemption is about being set free from our enslavement to this mortal coil, but it's not about escaping the physical realm. At our resurrection, the Lord Jesus will greet us with a new (physical) body fit for a new (physical) creation. However, it won't be just any human body. The promise is that we will be transformed into the likeness of Jesus' own resurrected body:

> But our citizenship is in heaven. And we eagerly await a Saviour from there, the Lord Jesus Christ, who, by the power that enables him to bring everything under his control, will transform our lowly bodies so that they will be like his glorious body. (Phil 3:20-21)

When you read the Gospel accounts of Jesus' post-resurrection appearances, you are staring at your own future. His empty tomb is your empty tomb. His resurrected body is a pattern for your resurrected body (Luke 24:39). Our suffering will then be over; we will leave this creation that is in bondage to decay, and we will finally leave this body that is constantly in a state of groaning.

Presently, this body is subject to decay, and all the fluoride in the world can't stop it. However, because we know our adoption and new body are coming, we wait patiently: "For in this hope we were saved. But hope that is seen is no hope at all. Who hopes for what they already have? But if we hope for what we do not yet have, we wait for it patiently" (Rom 8:24-25).

This future hope determines our present choices. Life works this way all the time. What prevented me from crossing the line sexually when I was engaged? Knowing that the wedding day was coming. There was going to be a honeymoon, so I could wait. What enables a child to be patient on a long car trip (at least in theory)? Knowing that the holiday house is getting closer.

What enables us to patiently endure suffering? Knowing the day of glory is coming.

It may be a hope that does not disappoint, but it is still a hope. In the Bible, hope is by definition a certain future outcome, not a present experience. And patience and endurance in suffering are the key signs that show you know you will be set free—the signs that you have *hope*.

So yes, we who have the Spirit groan—along with a creation that is groaning—but we groan with patient confidence and with certainty. More than that, in this present age we are comforted by the truth that we don't groan alone in our suffering.

The Spirit groans as he intercedes for us

> In the same way, the Spirit helps us in our weakness. We do not know what we ought to pray for, but the Spirit himself intercedes for us through wordless groans. (v. 26)

God has not abandoned his children to this broken world. Amidst the suffering, mindful of our weakness, wrapped in a world of futility and decay, trapped in a body that both suffers and resists the call to serve, we are left to groan. And at times our groans fail to turn themselves into prayer. Prayer itself becomes a matter of sitting before God with our pain, even when that pain sits there in us like a brick in the gut. Sometimes the best you can do is to be still and know that God is God (Ps 46:10). At times, we are so overwhelmed by the brokenness of this world that we don't know *how* to pray, and we don't know *what* to pray.

Into this pain and our struggle to pray, Romans 8 injects a ray of light. The same Spirit who sets us free to obey, the same Spirit who dwells within us, the same Spirit who adopts us and enables us to cry "Abba, Father"—this same Spirit actually groans *for us*.

Once again, God does what we can't do for ourselves. Just as Jesus shared our suffering, so the Spirit now shares our weakness, groaning and interceding for us. If it is still not yet clear to you that the Spirit is a person, surely this truth should confirm it once and for all. When we are totally helpless and utterly incapacitated, the Spirit takes our groans and turns our angst into 'class A' prayers. He takes our inarticulate grunts, and refashions them into prayers that are dead-on-target with God's will. He is able to do that because of his unique relationship with both the Father and with us: "And he who searches our hearts knows the mind of the Spirit, because the Spirit intercedes for God's people in accordance with the will of God" (Rom 8:27). The Son of God presents his blood on our behalf, and now the Spirit of God presents his prayers on our behalf. Even when we get it wrong, he makes it right.

The Spirit is the third member of the Trinity. As such, he knows the Father intimately, and is equally known by the Father (1 Cor 2:6-16). There are no secrets between them. The Spirit also knows everything about us, including the deepest groans of the people of God. It's that unique set of relationships which allows the Spirit to mediate for us in our pain.

In 2010, my church finally built our new multipurpose church building. After 20 years of using public buildings, it was a relief to finally locate our ministry in a safe and comfortable home. My fellow deacon and dear friend Shane worked on this project with me and the other deacons, Steve and Ed, over a period of ten years.

Just before we opened the building, Shane was diagnosed with cancer. He was given a life expectancy of two years; but it was only two months before he died. The only time Shane entered the new building was in a coffin, at age 43, leaving behind his wife, Amanda, and their six children. The funeral took place on my 50th birthday.

I was overwhelmed with grief and undiagnosed depression. For the next 18 months I went through the motions, often unable to be fully and emotionally present. I found it hard to stay focused on any project. For months I would often be woken from my sleep in tears as I recalled Shane's death. My prayer life was shot to pieces. I truly didn't know how to pray or what to pray. I ached with the deep, deep sorrow of loss.

Now imagine a conversation within the triune God about me during this time. The Spirit says to the Father: "Father, if Ray knew himself like I know him, then this is what he would want to say right now… And if Ray knew you like I know you, this is how he would say it…"[66]

Just the thought of the intercession of the Spirit moves me to tears. I was never alone through those dark days. The Spirit of Jesus had my back, and he has yours as well.

As you know, this is not in any way an encouragement to withhold casting your cares before your Father. It truly would be a tragedy to misread this truth and in so doing miss

---

[66] I am indebted to John Chapman, who is now groaning no more, for this insight.

out on the privileges and necessity of prayer. But you must know that, in the worst of times, when you lack clarity of thought or when your heart aches with pain, when you can't focus and you feel like you have nothing to say, the beautiful Spirit of God is saying it to the Father for you.

We groan for glory, we groan with confidence—and even as we groan, we know that the glory outstrips the suffering by a trillion to one. We groan knowing that we will not be mere spectators to the unveiling of glory, but we will be part of it, with glorified bodies fit for a new creation.

We groan patiently, and God in his kindness has not left us to groan alone.

For in the dark moments, when life is heavy, when the pain is as thick as custard, when the joy has passed and the tears come quickly, we have the Spirit of God taking our groans before the Father and turning them into prayers that are exactly what God wants to answer.

Comfort from the Spirit
Grant Dibden

It had been difficult for my wife, Jeanette, to fall pregnant, but after several years of waiting, tests and procedures, we did indeed have a baby boy. We named him Ian, which means 'gift of God', and we were very conscious that God had blessed us with him. He was happy, beautiful, and growing, and we loved being a young family.

A year later, Ian contracted bacterial meningitis.[67] In just a few days, Ian went from being a happy and busy little boy to being a bit unwell with a cold (we thought), to slipping into unconsciousness and being hospitalized. He was kept on life support until we were ready to say goodbye, and Ian died in our arms the day before his first birthday.

We had waited for so long for our baby and we loved him so much. We were broken-hearted.

Some wise friends, who had themselves miscarried twins, comforted us by saying, "Don't expect that you have to go through the classic seven stages of grieving. God may well deal gently with you." And that is what happened. And yet we had all the questions you would expect: If God could heal Ian, why didn't he? Were we being punished? Why did God allow this to happen?

But even in the midst of this loss and sadness, we noticed that we weren't despairing. As hard as it was, we were not without hope. Solid, certain hope came from God. It came from relying on God and his promises, even when things were very, very hard.

God also used wonderful Christian friends to comfort us. They cooked meals for us, visited us, talked and talked and talked with us, cried alongside us, and prayed with and for us. We know that the Holy Spirit intervened for us and turned our fumbling prayers into just the right prayers to our heavenly Father.

At Ian's funeral, Jeanette and I were both struck with the thought that God had lost his Son, but not because of

---

67 At the time there was no vaccine for this strain of meningitis (HIB), but a vaccine became available a few years later.

circumstances beyond his control. God's Son had been **given** in our place. This realization helped us trust God. We knew that if God had loved us enough to give up his Son for us, we still had great hope—hope that God was good; hope that God was in control (in ways that we didn't understand); and hope that Ian was in God's care in heaven.

In a time like that, God was the only one to whom we could turn, and he didn't let us down. As the years have gone by, the intensity of the pain has eased, but we still get emotional at certain times. We can testify that the Holy Spirit continues to comfort us by giving us the certain hope of being with God in eternity and being with our dear son Ian again.

10

God is in the thick of it
Romans 8:28-29

²⁸ And we know that **in all things God works for the good of those who love him**, who have been called according to his purpose. ²⁹ For those God foreknew he also predestined to be conformed to the image of his Son, that he might be the firstborn among many brothers and sisters. (Rom 8:28-29)

I remember seeing the band INXS at the Bondi Lifesaver's Club in the early 1980s. One of their first hits, 'The Loved One', had just been released, and they were the support band for the greatest band in the world, Cold Chisel. Michael Hutchence, the front man for INXS, was a man who lived up to the name of his band. Tragically, he died alone in his room at Sydney's Ritz-Carlton hotel in 1997, just 37 years old.

At Michael's funeral, his brother said that when they were much younger, Michael had made a list of ten things he wanted to achieve in his life. The first item on the list was to 'conquer the world'. He was clearly a man with big dreams, and he appeared to have accomplished that goal—or perhaps he was the one conquered by the demons that so often haunt the successful.

It may be the language of generals, kings and rock legends, but the language of 'conquering' is properly the language of the children of God: "No, in all these things we are more than conquerors through him who loved us" (8:37). Romans 8 begins with a strong declaration of assurance: "Therefore, there is now no condemnation for those who are in Christ Jesus" (v. 1). And it ends on an even stronger note of assurance, if that were possible, by telling us that "[nothing] in all creation, will be able to separate us from the love of God that is in Christ Jesus our Lord" (v. 39). Where it matters most, we who are in Christ Jesus conquer. In fact, we are "more than conquerors" because of the truths spelled out in verses 28 and 29, which announce the wonderful promise that *God will have his way in all things*.

God is working for our good

The verse voted most likely to be a comfort to Christians in hard times (and the verse most likely to be used by a preacher when he doesn't know how to apply an Old Testament passage) is Romans 8:28:

> And we know that in all things God works for the good of those who love him, who have been called according to his purpose.

The good news is that God is intimately involved with every part of our life. By "all things", Paul means the suffering and the persecution that seeks out the Christian, as well as all the pain that comes from living in a creation that is groaning. In the good and the bad, God is actively at work, and he is no passive bystander. As Jesus said, not one insignificant sparrow "will fall to the ground outside your Father's care" (Matt 10:29).

We can't pick and choose when God is sovereign. From the vantage point of the siege of Jerusalem in the Old Testament, when things were so unbearable that mothers were horrifically tempted to eat their young, we read these strong words:

> Who can speak and have it happen
>   if the Lord has not decreed it?
> Is it not from the mouth of the Most High
>   that both calamities and good things come?
> (Lam 3:37-38)

Speaking through the prophet Isaiah, God himself was clear about the extent of his sovereignty:

> "I form the light and create darkness,
>   I bring prosperity and create disaster;
>   I, the LORD, do all these things." (Isa 45:7)

Yet our verse in Romans says, "in *all things* God works for the good of those who love him".

There are two great temptations that come in the face of suffering. Both of them will make you want to give up and fall into despair. The first temptation is to think that God is not in control. When times of trouble come, it can appear comforting at first to believe that God has no part to play in the hard times. This was the conclusion of Rabbi Harold Kushner as he reflected on his son's tragic death. In Kushner's thinking, God was simply unable to prevent the loss of his son. He writes, "I can worship a God who hates suffering but cannot eliminate it, more easily than I can worship a God who chooses to make children suffer and die".[68] However, to take this position, we are forced to ignore consistent biblical teaching on the sovereignty of God. The result of this kind of thinking is that we make God in our own image, and he quickly becomes a god who is unworthy of our worship and unfit for our prayers. Moreover, if God's hands are in any way tied, then our life is at the mercy of either agents of evil, or of loveless, random chance in a profoundly lonely universe. But Romans 8:28 grounds our confidence in the profound truth that God actively works in all things.

The second temptation in the face of suffering is to believe that, yes, God is in control, but he is not working things out for our good. If this is the case, God cannot be trusted.

However, the promise in verse 28 is that God is working in all things (the things we call 'good' and the things we call 'bad') "for the good of those who love him". That is why we don't need to be conquered by doubts about God's love when suffering comes. We may not know why this quota of suffering came to this particular person at this particular time, but the call is to take God at his word and trust that he is intimately involved in our painful experiences, with the specific

---

68 Harold S Kushner, *When Good Things Happen to Bad People*, Schocken, New York, 1981, p. 134; quoted in DA Carson, *How Long, O Lord? Reflections on Suffering and Evil*, Baker, Grand Rapids, 1990, p. 29.

intent of doing good to his people. Only then will suffering achieve God's purpose. Only then will suffering make us better, not bitter. This radical truth speaks to any misguided doubt that our suffering is motivated by some divine hatred; it is for our good, and not for our harm.

In this fallen creation, God is uniquely glorified when his people journey through pain and yet lay claim to God's goodness. This happens when we live by faith, not by sight (2 Cor 5:7). We live by a faith that cannot see clearly now, but will one day see that God is supremely good, and that the perseverance of the saints was truly worth it. As theologian Don Carson states, "That sort of promise has to be taken on faith—faith that is strong because of the proof God has already given us of his love for us, the proof that is nothing less than the gift of his Son".[69]

To whom does this wonderful promise apply? To be sure, suffering has shaped the character of many humans outside of the circle of faith. For others, it's been the launch pad into unbelief. As Australian rock legend Jimmy Barnes (the lead singer of my beloved Cold Chisel) reflects on his very poor upbringing in Glasgow and Australia, he writes, "It seems we would have to fight against God and the elements for our home and our happiness. I was really starting to dislike this God character I kept hearing about. He didn't seem to do anything for anybody, especially the people we knew. Maybe we didn't deserve his help." Later in his biography he writes, "I had by this time come to the conclusion that there was no God. I knew it wasn't anything like they told me in Sunday School. There was no-one looking down on us from above

69 Carson, *How Long, O Lord?*, pp. 26-7.

and there was no heaven and no hell." And yet in his preface, Jimmy ironically affirms, "I always feel I had luck on my side, someone looking over my shoulder, keeping an eye out for me".[70]

For so many, suffering produces an atheistic sense of 'fate', not joyful perseverance. The promise in Romans 8:28 that has comforted so many is reserved for those who love God, who are drawn to him by his irresistible and gracious call, and who live by faith, not by sight.

Paul has already introduced us to the surprising value of suffering earlier in Romans. In chapter 5, the apostle explains why God's people can glory in their sufferings: "because we know that suffering produces perseverance; perseverance, character; and character, hope. And hope does not put us to shame…" (vv. 3-5). In the midst of temporal pain, there remains an eternal promise. Suffering unleashes a set of character-shaping experiences that stimulate certain hope. In short, suffering unbolts the door of the heart and allows the eternal promises of God to find their mark deep within one's soul. Suffering makes us hungry for a heaven that will not disappoint.

It's also vital that we're clear on the nature of the 'good' that is promised. For some, this verse functions like a Christian version of a rabbit's foot or a lucky charm: "Nothing bad can ever happen to me, because I'm protected by Romans 8:28". The 'good', however, is not some promise of a pain-free lifestyle with a guaranteed quota of maximum pleasure, where every boy or girl you ask out says yes, where you come first in

---

[70] Jimmy Barnes, *Working Class Boy*, Harper Collins, Sydney, 2016, pp. x, 78, 147-8.

every exam you sit, where you succeed every time you apply for a job, and where every business venture you embark on is a winner. Paul has already made it perfectly clear that life in this cursed world carries with it a measure of suffering, just as our Saviour and brother suffered (e.g. 8:17-21).

In fact, the very next verse gives us a clear definition of what God sees as the 'good':

> For those God foreknew he also predestined **to be conformed to the image of his Son**, that he might be the firstborn among many brothers and sisters. (v. 29)

'The good' is us becoming more like Christ

So God's sovereign plan, which stretches back to before the beginning of time, plays out in every experience of life. God's stubborn goal in any and every experience is that you will be transformed into the image of the Lord Jesus, who is pictured here as your older brother.

God sent his own Son in the likeness of sinful man (v. 3) so that we would be conformed to the likeness of the Son (v. 29), so that Christ ushers in a new family where his brothers and sisters resemble him more and more. This is what I call legitimate Christian cloning.

This promise still doesn't explain why suffering is unevenly handed out; however, it does explain how God wants us to respond to every experience that comes our way. God's great call for you is not to be a doctor or a computer programmer, or to marry a specific man, or to live in a particular house. God has called you simply and profoundly to be holy. To be more specific, he has called you to be more like Jesus to the glory of God. There is no greater good on offer. Every experience in your life is entrusted to you so that you might become more like the Son of God. This goal to be Christlike in all things is for both the individual Christian and the church as a whole.

This is such a radical proposition. What it means is that God can work 'good' in the midst of your husband leaving you, or your wife telling you she is not a Christian after your first year of being married. The 'good' is not that you will get the job, or develop a skill, or avoid the criticism, or escape the depression (economic or emotional). In all things, God's good purpose for us is that we will reflect the beauty of the character of the Saviour.

One of my great Christian heroes is Helen Roseveare. Helen passed away in late 2016, but spent many years as an overseas missionary. In 1964, she was serving as a missionary doctor in the Congo, and found herself caught up in the Simba rebellion (part of the Congo Crisis of the early 1960s). During the uprising, rebel soldiers killed over 100,000 people. Many Christian missionaries were raped and killed, and Helen was one of those who were sexually abused.

Looking back many years later, Helen reflected on what she'd felt as she was taken away to be raped. She said she'd felt as though God was saying to her, "Can you thank me for trusting you with this experience, even if I never tell you why?"[71]

---

71   Helen Roseveare, 'Why Does a God of Love Allow Suffering', interview with Moira Brown on *100 Huntley Street*, part 2 at 2:45, Crossroads Christian Communications, Burlington, Ontario (viewed 18 April 2017): www.100huntley.com/watch?id=216538&title=why-does-a-god-of-love-allow-suffering-2.

This in no way diminishes the evil of the sin, nor the culpability of the persons inflicting the sin, but it does mean that the sin will not have the final victory. It's hard to believe how this dear woman could speak in such faith-stretching ways. Clearly, she trusted God to entrust this awful experience to her, and in so doing Helen was like her Lord Jesus, who entrusted himself to the sovereign will of his Father (1 Pet 2:23).

Romans 8:28 highlights this one profound truth: in every moment of every day, we are encountering God's sovereign hand. God is involved in every situation—good or bad, large or small—without in any way being the author of sin. This means that the next time a hurtful word comes your way, the next time you find yourself exasperated by another person, the next time you experience injustice or a loss, remember God is in the thick of it. He is saying, "I am entrusting this experience to you to shape you to be more like my Son".

To put it another way, God is into recycling. Wikipedia defines recycling as "the process of converting waste materials into new materials and objects".[72] God is the master recycler. He recycles our pain and turns it into the fruit of the Spirit for his glory. Nothing is wasted.

Take a moment to personally reflect on the last time you responded to some situation in an ungodly way—whether it was sulking, sarcasm, or some cynical or critical remark. Now pause and ask yourself the question: "What did you want that you did not get?" Was it order, perfection, control, peace, respect, love, quiet, honour, praise, or simply

---

[72] 'Recycling', *Wikipedia.org*, 22 May 2017 (viewed 12 June 2017): www.wikipedia.org/wiki/Recycling.

for the lawnmower to start? Now ask the next question: "Ultimately, whose decision was it to not give you the thing that you sought, and why?"

Romans 8:28-29 reminds us that God is fully engaged in every event in your life—from being stuck in traffic or dealing with a critical comment, right through to the very serious type of suffering that Helen Roseveare faced. God is in the thick of it. He is using every experience to shape us to be more like Christ. And remember, this is the same Christ who had the right to be angry when he faced unjust suffering, but instead prayed, "Father, forgive them, for they do not know what they are doing" (Luke 23:34). This means that the very things and the very people whom we think cause our anger, sarcasm and sulking are there under God's providence to teach us to be slow to anger, patient, gentle and kind. Who would have thought? The same people and situations that we blame to justify our sinful responses are the very same people and situations that God uses to shape us to be more like his Son—if only we would let him. This is the 'good' of verse 28, and it will not happen automatically. It will not happen without a quota of pain and tears. But in the providence of God, it will happen.

I recall the words of that 14-year-old boy from our church, Jake, who, as I mentioned earlier, had severely damaged his spine. Apart from a miracle, he was going to be a quadriplegic. Five weeks after an operation, at 3am, in the midst of a night of pain, he looked at his mother and said, "Mum, if it took me breaking my neck for you to become a Christian, it was worth it". So much suffering, and yet God was right there in the thick of it, working out his purposes and bringing so much good, through many tears and through bucketloads of prayer.

Malcolm Muggeridge, a former atheist and journalist who later became a Christian, once said, "Everything of value I've ever learned in life has been through suffering".[73] Perhaps this is an overstatement. God does work in all things, even in the pleasures of life. And yet if you reflect on your own spiritual journey, you will probably find that the great moments of insight and deep conviction have usually come through suffering. The reason is simple: "We know that suffering produces perseverance; perseverance, character; and character, hope" (Rom 5:3b-4).

Elisabeth Elliot, author and two-time widow, testifies to this comfort when she writes:

> I am not a theologian or a scholar, but I am very aware of the fact that pain is necessary to all of us. In my own life, I think I can honestly say that out of the deepest pain has come the strongest conviction of the presence of God and the love of God.[74]

This journey does not happen overnight. Often we need some emotional distance from our suffering to create the space that allows us to think God's thoughts after him. Many times, all we have is the cry "How Long, O Lord?"—and perhaps for you, now is that time. But if you're able, why not stop reading at this point and recall the three worst events in your life? Spend some time prayerfully pondering whether Helen Roseveare, Malcolm Muggeridge and Elisabeth Elliot have a point.

---

73 Quoted in Paul E Little, *Know Why You Believe*, 4th edn, IVP, Downers Grove, 2000, p. 180.
74 Quoted in Samuel R Chand, *Leadership Pain*, Thomas Nelson, Nashville, 2015, p. 6.

A lifeline of hope

Wendy Potts

I pray that God would give me a heart attack so I don't have to endure this any longer.

I just don't want to be here any more. I can't do this any longer.

These are the awful cries of my husband's heart that I have heard far too often. In the last few years, there are days and weeks where he hangs on by a thread. Not that it is obvious to those around us. It is mostly an invisible illness.

Dark days. Long nights. Lonely years.

It's been 18 years since Shaun's health took a dive—a dive that hit the rocks. We remember the day well. On New Year's Day in 1999, he awoke covered in chicken pox spots. It was the worst case I'd seen, but of course at that stage we had no idea that he would never recover. He was 33. Most viruses hit hard and move on after a few days, weeks, or months at the most. This one hit his immune system like a tonne of bricks and left him debilitatingly tired for years. Tired doesn't begin to capture it; "like swimming through concrete" is how he explains the feeling. Too tired to work in the ministry that he was passionate about. Too tired to sit on the sideline of the kids' soccer games. Too tired to attend church. For years, too tired to come downstairs for dinner. Even, at times, too tired to read or to talk!

On top of that, he experienced a muscle pain that kept him up at night and demanded heavy drugs just to endure heat, light, noise, stress and chemical sensitivities. All this has worsened and Shaun has been pretty well housebound for years now. He goes between being upstairs in the bedroom and downstairs in the office (on a good day).

Shaun's condition has been labelled 'CFIDS' (Chronic Fatigue Immune Dysfunction Syndrome). It is like drowning in a whirlpool that never ends and is so bad that, at times, he looks on jealously at those with a terminal illness. The comfort and hope of the resurrection body is sometimes itself a temptation to take matters into his own hands.

Dark days. Long nights. Lonely years.

I don't share our story to make you feel sorry for us, because our story is merely a sample of the untold suffering of so many others. I write (with Shaun's permission, and because he can't) in the hope that you will take encouragement from the way God has kept him (and us) going through our suffering. He has done this through "the surpassing worth of knowing Christ Jesus [our] Lord" (Phil 3:8).

The grief has taken different forms over the years, as have the lessons, the provisions, and the comfort of God. Ultimately, it is the hope that we have in Jesus that makes all the difference to our survival! We have had to cling to this hope, as the losses seem to cover every area of our life.

Loss of health: The contrast was enormous. Shaun used to charge through life at 1000%. He was a picture of fitness—a big-wave surfer, black-run skier, 4-day mountain hiker, and collector of Bear Grylls-style 'near-death experiences' involving snakes, spiders and big waves. He was a commercial-builder-turned-ordained-minister-and-itinerant evangelist—a man whose diary left people breathless, with over 300 engagements a year around the country. He was a fit and gifted young man with a young family and a promising ministry future.

Loss of ministry and purpose: "The LORD gave and the LORD has taken away" (Job 1:21). Shaun was always quick to say that his ministry was God-given kingdom work—and that God didn't need him to do it. He knew from day one that he was not irreplaceable. He knew that his gifts in evangelism and preaching, his energy and passion, had come from God. He knew straight-up that he had no rights to claim anything from God. God owed him nothing. And yet he felt the loss of what God had given and then taken away. It didn't make sense to any of us that he was taken out of action mid-game. But then, when does tragedy ever make sense to us?

Loneliness: Shaun's world has become smaller and smaller. CFIDS is very isolating. The sense of abandonment is strong. Surprisingly, good friends have become strangers who keep their distance (even as, wonderfully, strangers became good friends). It is confronting to visit someone who is getting worse. And all too often, God feels like a stranger. Psalm 22 echoes the cries of the heart: "My God, my God, why have you forsaken me? Why are you so far from saving me, so far from my cries of anguish?" The lack of understanding, especially from those closest to you, is painful. Frequently it seems that even I am the cause of such emotional pain.

Anger: Recognizing and then managing our anger at each other, at life, and at God has been a long road. Resentment builds walls that, if unforgiven, turn into impassable borders.

Loss of marriage and family life: Our two little boys were two years old and three months old when Shaun first got sick.

It was a crazy and exhausting time. Five years later, we took the plunge and had a baby girl. I am not an authentic single mum—but most of the time I feel like one. The bulk of parenting and managing the household, ferrying kids around and financial support is up to me. Sometimes Shaun is emotionally available, and at other times he simply isn't. It's not his fault, but often I blame him. Sometimes I run away from him in my heart. It is not my fault, but often he blames me.

Sometimes the thread gets very thin. I can understand how people leave. There have been desperate times when leaving has been the only way ahead that I can see. But each time, Jesus brings us through the darkness.

By the grace of God, we are still together. But for me, the emotional pain of 'losing' my husband is the hardest thing to bear. He is not the same man I married. I guess that is why the promise 'for better, for worse… in sickness and in health' is so profound, and why the clause "with God's help" is so vital. God has provided light in the darkness in the form of wise counsel, dear friends to weep and pray with, the loving provision for our needs, the provision of repentance, forgiveness and compassion when the well is dry, and the spiritual reminder that when my husband is unable to be a husband to me, ultimately Jesus is my 'husband'.

God has given us the determination and resolve to start again—again and again. And he has given us the unshakeable Scriptures, which remind us of God's presence, God's promises and God's power, even when we don't feel those things.

We often say that one day we might look back from heaven's perspective and, like Paul in 2 Corinthians 1, see how the prayers of the saints have delivered us (2 Cor 1:10-11).

We are wowed by those who have prayed for us weekly for years now—some friends, some strangers I've never met.

Romans 8:28-29 is the passage we love above all others. It is like a lifeline of hope.

- *All things:* God promises that he will use all of it. Though much of it is our junk, none of it is wasted.
- *For our good:* He is good, and his plans for us are good.
- *Called according to his purpose:* This was never our plan or purpose, but it is his. CFIDS has taken us by surprise, but it is not a detour or a roadblock. It is the main road because it is God's road.
- *Predestined:* God is in charge. He who called us will keep us. What great security is found in that!
- *Conformed to the image of his Son:* our greatest good is to become more like Jesus. I'm not brave enough to pray, "Whatever it takes, Lord". But I can trust that he is doing that in our lives.

11

Thinking really big picture
Romans 8:29-30

²⁹ **For those God foreknew he also predestined** to be conformed to the image of his Son, that he might be the firstborn among many brothers and sisters. ³⁰ And those he predestined, **he also called**; those he called, **he also justified**; those he justified, **he also glorified**. (Rom 8:29-30)

Last Christmas, my daughter received a 1000-piece jigsaw puzzle. She has recently completed it, much to the relief of the rest of the family, who may once again use our coffee table. The completed picture was a beautiful collage of Disney characters. But imagine trying to take one piece of the puzzle and work out the broader picture just by looking at that one piece—it would be impossible.

You can see where this illustration is heading.

We cannot make sense of our existence and the suffering we experience if all we have is our single piece of the puzzle.

Our lives need to be placed in a much wider context, or the things that happen to us will remain a never-ending mystery.

We will only grasp that God works in every situation for our good if we locate every experience in our lives within God's eternal purposes. As we will see, these purposes stretch back from before creation and look forward to our glorious future. We need to see everything in our lives within this big picture, and Romans 8:29-30 gives us five key words that paint God's really big picture—five words capturing five undeniable truths, which together tell the story of salvation from God's perspective. This is the one history lesson you really need to learn. As you ponder these five words, you notice that it's about 'He' before it's about 'Me'. The big picture is radically God-centred.

Five undeniable truths

1. Foreknew

> "For those God *foreknew*…"

This golden chain of blessings begins before the creation of the world. Before time itself, God entered into a relationship with his people. To 'foreknow' is, very simply, to know beforehand. In the Bible, the verb 'to know' is generally a relational concept involving much more than simple information and data. So God's foreknowledge is about much more than God knowing about us, or knowing in advance what we're going to do. It's about God relationally knowing *us* since before the creation of the world.

In Amos 3:2, God says of Israel, "You only have I chosen

[foreknown] of all the families of the earth". While God is omniscient and so knows all things, including every detail of every nation, he only 'knew'—or entered into a covenantal relationship with—Israel. He set his affection on this nation alone. This explains why the NIV translates Amos 3:2 as "You only have I chosen" even though a more literal translation would simply use the word 'known'.

So the language of foreknowledge that was first applied to Israel, the chosen nation, in the Old Testament is now applied to those who are in Christ, the chosen people of God in the new covenant.

2. Predestined

"For those God foreknew he also *predestined*..."

There is that scary word: predestination!

As we begin thinking about this idea, it's important to note that 'predestination' is a biblical word, not a theological word like 'Trinity'.[75] That is, it's a word used in the Bible. And it means what it says—that God determined the destiny of his people before (pre) time. Their destiny is that they would be called, justified, and glorified. In other words, they would be co-heirs with Christ and would share in both his suffering and his glory.

---

75 In describing 'Trinity' as a 'theological word', I don't mean that 'predestination' and other biblical words are somehow *un*theological. I simply mean that 'Trinity' is a word introduced by theologians to capture biblical teaching and biblical concepts, even though the word itself doesn't appear in the pages of the Bible. Clearly, 'predestination' is a biblical word *and* a theological word.

Every Christian believes that they choose God, and every Christian believes that God chooses them. But these two words, 'foreknew' and 'predestined', remind us that we chose God only because he first chose us in Christ. Elsewhere, Paul describes our salvation this way: "In love he predestined us for adoption to sonship through Jesus Christ" (Eph 1:4-5).

Why is it that most women (and some men) love getting flowers from their loved ones? Let's face it—it's not all that practical. The flowers cost money, in three days they begin to shrivel, and they are eventually thrown away (as my wife tells me, this is especially the case if the flowers are bought from a service station). However, I think part of the joy of receiving flowers is in the recipient knowing that, in the midst of their lover's busy day, he or she stopped and thought about doing good to their lover.

Before time began, God stopped, turned his attention to you, and said, "I want to do good to you. You will be coming home with me on the last day." It was a unilateral decision, not unlike a planned marriage—and, as you may know, planned marriages tend to be more successful!

Significantly, he did this without regard to any worthiness on the part of those he chose. The decision to choose us is driven not by the worthiness of the recipient, but by the love of God in Christ. As Paul states in Romans 9 when using the example of twin brothers Jacob and Esau (from Genesis 25), God chose Jacob over Esau "before the twins were born or had done anything good or bad, in order that God's purpose in election might stand: not by works but by him who calls…" (Rom 9:11-12). God's election is without any regard to the worthiness of the one chosen: "It does not, therefore, depend on human desire or effort, but on God's mercy" (9:16). Predestination emphatically declares that our salvation is all grace from start to finish.[76]

3. Called

"And those he predestined, he also *called*…"

Paul's use of 'call' here is different from the universal call of the gospel, in which all people everywhere are invited to repent and come to Christ through faith. In this verse, Paul refers to the idea that at a certain point in the life of every Christian, God puts into effect his decision to choose that person. He does it not simply by inviting them objectively in the preaching of the gospel, but by summoning them subjectively to himself through his Spirit. The hour he called you was the very same hour you believed.[77] You call on the name of the Lord only because he first called you—because the Father gave you his Spirit to draw you to his Son and to enable you to call on him as Lord (Rom 5:5; 1 Cor 12:3). Yet he did it in such a way that wooed your will, rather than destroying it.

For Paul, God's call is an irresistible command. There has never been a person who was predestined who fails to make it to the end of the 'golden chain', where they are glorified. Jesus himself speaks of his Father's 'drawing' those who are his to the Son (John 6:44), and Jesus revealing his Father to those whom he chooses (Matt 11:27).

---

76 See appendix C for further reflections on predestination.
77 As Spurgeon wisely said, just as you don't need to remember the day of your birth to know you're alive, so you don't need to know the day you were born again to know that you are alive in Christ.

There are none who are lost between those God foreknew, those God called, and those God will glorify. They are exactly the same group of people. God's plan is invincible, and he will have his way. God works in all things, including everything needed to accomplish our salvation.

4. Justified

"those he called, he also *justified*..."

The language of justification comes from the courtroom. To be justified means that God the judge declares us to be righteous on the basis of Jesus' death and resurrection on our behalf. The ones to whom God grants the gift of faith and repentance are declared to be as righteous as Christ himself. It is a righteousness that is given as a gift. As a result, we in Christ are fully pardoned and set free from even a hint of condemnation. You may find it helpful to think of being justified as being treated '*just* (as) *if I'd* never sinned'. As Paul writes in Romans 5:1, "Therefore, since we have been justified through faith, we have peace with God through our Lord Jesus Christ". In Christ, you can know *now* what God is going to say about you on the last day: "Not guilty!"

This is where those of us who are in Christ now stand. We are, as it were, four-fifths of our way into God's story. Within the chain of blessings, we are sandwiched between being justified now and eagerly awaiting the glory to come. And as we wait, God is using all things to conform us to the image of his Son.

5. Glorified

"those he justified, he also *glorified*."

The big surprise here is that we are described as already being glorified. Our glorification is seen as being *past* tense, not future tense.

So far in Romans 8, Paul has described our glory in terms of a future experience that we 'eagerly await'. God, however, loves to talk about things that will happen in the future as if they have already happened, because when you are dealing with a sovereign God the outcome is certain. Those God foreknew before the foundation of the earth are those who will be glorified at the end of time—and there is absolutely no doubt about it!

Can you sense that God wants to pack as much assurance into your Christian life as you can tolerate? He does that by accentuating his sovereign grace—by showing you that your salvation is all from him, from first to last. For only then will God receive the glory that is rightfully his.

Is God unjust?

If you've understood what has been said, then you will realize that God has chosen and predestined some, but not all. As a Christian, you're part of the privileged few.

My daughter first grasped the implications of this truth when she was 12 years old. She was sitting in the back seat of a car, travelling up the east coast of Tasmania. Her first reaction was, "That sucks!" Her mind was racing—not in the direction of gratitude, but in the direction of her friends whom she now realized may not be predestined.

When predestination is correctly taught, it provokes two questions. Thankfully for us, Paul anticipates and answers both these questions in Romans 9: "Is God unjust?" (v. 14) and "Why does God still blame us, for who is able to resist his will?" (v. 19). These are good questions, and they are my questions.[78] Sometimes I, too, feel as if this is unfair. But at the end of the day, we are left with one question: "Will we let God be God?"

The answer Paul gives to the first question is to quote God's statement to Moses in the Old Testament book of Exodus: "I will have mercy on whom I have mercy, and I will have compassion on whom I have compassion" (Rom 9:15; cf. Exod 33:19). Paul's answer to the second question almost contains a note of defiance: "But who are you, a human being, to talk back to God?" (Rom 9:20).

Before the days of GPS and Google Maps, every car would carry around a book called a street directory. You could go to the back of that book to find the street and suburb you were looking for by following the relevant coordinates and page number. However, at the very back of each street directory was a page titled 'end of map'. It was a reminder that there was a limit to what the street directory could tell you. It wasn't as if there were no more streets, but those streets were beyond the scope of this particular street directory.

Romans 9:20 tells us that we are at the end of map, the end of revelation on this topic.

We humans are tempted to demand more answers, rather than allowing God to set the limits on his revelation to us. We

---

78 For further reflections on these issues, see appendix C.

don't have the right to know everything about everything. Or perhaps we're tempted to domesticate God and make him conform to our sense of justice, rather than shouting out praise for his love and mercy.

As we come to the end of what God has revealed to us about this issue, it is very important to remember that *before* Paul explains God's sovereign grace in election in Romans 8 and 9, he goes to great pains to point out that at the cross God's justice (Rom 3:25-26) and God's love (Rom 5:8-10) are publicly demonstrated to every generation. God has displayed his love to the world by giving us his best (his Son) when we were at our worst (sinners and enemies of God). The worst thing a person can have in life is an enemy, and the best thing a person can give is one's life. These two things never go together—except that, on the first Good Friday, they did. God's love is beyond dispute.

Equally, God is so committed to not only being just but also being seen to be just that he had his one and only Son executed in public. He did this so the world would know that God will never forgive a sin that he has not already punished in the body of his Son. His mercy is not at the expense of his justice. This makes clear to every generation that God is right to declare us right, even when we are so wrong (Rom 3:26).

In the end, it is because of the cross that God expects us to be able to live with legitimate yet unanswered questions on election. We have more than enough evidence to know that God is good and just, and that God is love.

Walter Isaacson's biography of Steve Jobs records a beautiful moment from when Jobs was six or seven years old. He tells a girl who lived across the street that he was adopted:

"So does that mean your real parents didn't want you?" the girl asked. "Lightning bolts went off in my head," according to Jobs. "I remember running into the house, crying. And my parents said, 'No, you have to understand.' They were very serious and looked me straight in the eye. They said, '*We specifically picked you out.*' Both of my parents said that and repeated it slowly for me. And they put an emphasis on every word in that sentence."[79]

If you're a Christian, God is saying to you right now, "I specifically picked you out before time began!"

If you're not sure whether God is really saying this to you or whether you're one of the elect, go back to Romans 1. Remember that the gospel is the good news concerning Jesus Christ our Lord—news that is powerful to save *all* those who believe (Rom 1:16). The questions 'Do I believe in Jesus?' and 'Am I predestined?' are two sides of the same coin. To say 'yes' to one is to say 'yes' to the other. It may help to picture it this way: it's as though the front door of salvation quotes Jesus' words from Matthew 11:28: "Come to me, all you who are weary and burdened, and I will give you rest". Once a person enters through the door, however, he or she looks back and sees these words of Jesus written on the inside of the door: "For many are invited, but few are chosen" (Matt 22:14).

It is far more productive to focus on asking, 'Am I trusting in Jesus as my Lord and Saviour?' And if our trust is in Jesus, the idea of predestination brings the comfort and joy of knowing we are saved because God chose us. The gospel

---

79 Isaacson, *Steve Jobs*, p. 4; emphasis added.

saves, but your predestination will make sure you don't miss out on that salvation.

God's freewill or ours?

However, all this begs the question: Do humans have a real will?

The Bible is clear that we do make real choices, and we are held responsible for our choices (John 12:37). The Scriptures repeatedly call on us to exercise our will, to believe, and to repent. But, as we have already seen, human will in the flesh cannot and will not please God. Left to ourselves, we would never come to Christ (John 12:39).

So, we are left with another question: Who really has free will? Is it God, or is it humans?

If we believe that human beings have ultimate free will, then we must also believe that God does *not* have free will. He is beholden to our free choices. In the end, someone has to be in charge, and it's either God or us. It simply can't be both. So whom would we rather have behind the steering wheel? If we answer 'humanity', then we haven't understood either our own hearts or God's goodness and glory. If we insist that we have free will and we are the masters of our own destiny, we take 'free will' away from God.

But what a comfort it is to know that God is in charge of our salvation.

I remember the day that my friend's parents went to church for the very first time. Although both parents were atheists, they decided to graciously accept their daughter's persistent and earnest invitations, which she had given over five long years. It was Easter Sunday, so naturally the sermon was going to be about the resurrection of our Lord Jesus—what could go wrong? What went wrong was that the minister must have woken up in a bad mood, because he decided to criticize people who only attend church at Easter and Christmas. My friend's parents decided that day never to return to church again.

When I was told the story, I leaned forward and said to my friend, "Anne, isn't it good that we believe in predestination? Imagine if the salvation of our loved ones was in the hands of such fools like us."

The idea that God is sovereign is clearly countercultural, especially given that the highest good according to Western society is human freedom. However, the highest good according to Scripture is God's glory. God's purpose in election is to do that which most glorifies God. As Paul notes in Romans 9:23, God executes his plans "to make the riches of his glory known to the objects of his mercy, whom he prepared in advance for glory" (Rom 9:23).

If we rob God of his free will, we have robbed him of his gracious sovereignty, thus denying that he works in "all things". In the process, we've robbed ourselves of the comfort of knowing that our salvation rests ultimately in the hands of God. And if everything (including the salvation of our loved ones) is not under his full control, we've rendered God unfit to hear our prayers.

It is solely on the basis of God's sovereign free will that we are "more than conquerors" (8:37), because "if God is for us, who can be against us?" (8:31).

When confronted with election, many want to say, "It's not fair!" But the challenge for us is this: Do we want to spend the rest of our Christian life complaining that God is not who we want him to be? Or do we want to praise God and receive the comfort that his sovereign grace is intended to provide? The Bible urges us to respond to God's election by praising the God and Father of our Lord Jesus Christ. Likewise, our daily prayers should be filled with a never-ending refrain: "Thank you, thank you, thank you, Lord!"

So, when was the last time you gave thanks to God for choosing you in Christ Jesus?

That is certainly what Paul does in his extended prayer of praise in Ephesians 1:3-14, where he lists God's spiritual blessings in Christ: beginning with the fact that God "chose" us and "predestined" us in Christ Jesus.

Why do we think we are wiser than God when we ignore this praise point?

Why do we think we are more merciful than God by thinking that, if we were him, we would choose everyone?

As part of my weekly prayer points, I have a regular list of topics for praise and thanksgiving. Every Tuesday, I specifically thank God for choosing me. Why not make the same truth part of your regular prayers? Praise God that he is sovereign, and that in his sovereign mercy he foreknew us, predestined us, called us, justified us, and glorified us!

Accepted as a child of God
Steve Jeffrey

I remember my first couple of years as a Christian vividly; a mixture of joy like I'd never experienced and the deepest grief I'd ever experienced. I was torn between the joy of acceptance by God and the pain of rejection by the people closest to me: my family.

I grew up in what appeared to be a totally normal, God-fearing family. Jesus, the Bible, prayer, church and Christian morality were part of our family life. We were a very close-knit family. Then something went wrong with church. I was too young to know what, but conflicts arose between my parents and members of churches we attended. Conflicts tended to follow us from church to church. They seemed to be a constant presence in my formative years, turning into hostilities and vitriol towards some. Friends became enemies. Former childhood friends were not to be associated with. I didn't understand.

By the time I was a teenager, we had withdrawn from all church involvement. My family seemed to harbour a deep hostility towards the established church and those who were part of it. Their negative experience of church life had rubbed off on me.

So, humanly speaking, it's inexplicable that as a 22-year-old, I decided to drive for half an hour to attend church one Sunday morning. I knew it would be an unpopular decision, and it was. As time went on it became increasingly difficult to attend church and midweek Bible study. The 'silent treatment' was hard, the arguments even harder. I was deeply conflicted between the growing hostility of those closest to me, and the people who showed me kindness at church. I was conflicted between the things I was reading in the Bible about the characteristics of Jesus' disciples and my own life, and my experience of my family life.

My life of Bible reading, prayer and morality led me to a life of legalism and self-righteousness. I had little love for others and no relationship with God. I had no assurance that God had any goodwill towards me. I thought the best option was to go to a conference to find out how to be a missionary because then God would definitely be pleased with me. But on 30 April 1993, my life changed forever. I understood salvation by grace through the death and resurrection of Jesus for the first time in my life. I had found purpose and security.

Although my understanding of the Christian gospel was weak, assurance, joy and clarity about what mattered in life flooded in over the coming weeks. I came to understand that it wasn't by chance that I was in that room on April 30th; God had made it happen. It still overwhelms me to think that God had worked all things in my life to bring about his plan of salvation for me before he even made the universe. I'm a 'big picture' person, and that picture exploded my categories.

My assumption, upon returning home, was that I was the reason there had been so much tension between my parents and me. Given that I had only just discovered the good news of the Christian message, I thought the problems of the past were about me not getting it. I hoped the tension would now be a thing of the past. I was wrong. The tensions escalated, but I should have seen it coming. I was now more committed to God's people than ever. I was making decisions about church that were the total opposite of what my family wanted.

It wasn't long before I was working part-time at church, training for vocational ministry. For me, this is where the hostility grew beyond comprehension. I realized I was now being treated as an enemy. For two years of ministry training, the hostility with my parents was a dark cloud that hung over me every day. I felt manipulated and controlled. I dreaded stepping out in public for fear of being abused. I even feared physical assault after receiving veiled threats from extended family—at one point the police were involved. Family and many others pulled away, and so did I. There was one phone call that broke my heart: my father said to me, "As far as I'm concerned, you don't exist". That was the beginning of no contact for the next 13 years. They missed so many highlights in my life: graduation from theological college, ordination as a minister, marriage, and the birth of two children.

Very few people understood what I was going through. A fellow theological student even accused me of being at fault for the breakdown of relationship; he didn't believe my story. Other Christians affirmed the courage I had shown to follow Jesus, regardless of the cost.

But God wasn't finished with me or with my family. Disturbingly, the breakdown in my relationship with my parents became a badge of honour for me—a signpost of personal sacrifice that I could point to as evidence of my walk with God. Deep down, I was comfortable with the relationship staying as it was. I was settled. But God wasn't. His plan is to conform me to the image of his Son, and he worked in me to make me see how much I still needed to change. The gospel of reconciliation that I preached needed to be practised. He impressed Matthew 18 (the parable of the unmerciful servant) deep into my heart. My sin against God was so much greater than my parents' sin against me—and I needed to see and feel that. Otherwise, I would always dishonour my parents in the way I spoke about them and treated them.

After months of reflection, I realized I needed to take responsibility for three aspects of the breakdown of the relationship, all to do with not honouring my parents as I should have. With my security in God's acceptance of me in Christ, and a desire to be more like Jesus—and yet with a real fear of further rejection—I made a time to go and see them and confess.

I write my story for publication with their permission. It's actually our story. God was using our sin and brokenness and hostility and turning it around for his glory. When I started to speak to my parents, we all broke down in tears and confessed error. To my delight, God foreknew them too. They were part of a church and were being conformed to the image of his Son.

A couple of months later, they came to meet my wife and children for the first time. On the second night, my parents told me how proud they were of me as a man, a husband, a father, and a pastor. Truth be told, I had been hoping my whole life to hear those words, especially from my dad. My wife asked me later that night: "How did that make you feel?" My reply? It was wonderful to hear it, and great for them to have said it, but I didn't *need* it. The one thing I've wanted to hear all my life, I no longer need to hear. I realized in that moment how God had used such a terrible situation with my parents to give me such affirmation as his child.

12

What then shall we say in response?

Romans 8:31-39

³¹ What, then, shall we say in response to these things? If God is for us, who can be against us? ³² He who did not spare his own Son, but gave him up for us all—how will he not also, along with him, graciously give us all things? ³³ Who will bring any charge against those whom God has chosen? It is God who justifies. ³⁴ Who then is the one who condemns? No-one. Christ Jesus who died—more than that, who was raised to life—is at the right hand of God and is also interceding for us. ³⁵ Who shall separate us from the love of Christ? Shall trouble or hardship or persecution or famine or nakedness or danger or sword? ³⁶ As it is written:

> "For your sake we face death all day long;
> we are considered as sheep to be slaughtered."

⁣³⁷ No, **in all these things we are more than conquerors through him who loved us**. ³⁸ For I am convinced that neither death nor life, neither angels nor demons, neither the present nor the future, nor any powers, ³⁹ neither height nor depth, nor anything else in all creation, will be able to separate us from the love of God that is in Christ Jesus our Lord.

Romans 8 opens on a glorious note of assurance: "Therefore, there is now no condemnation for those who are in Christ Jesus" (v. 1). And our chapter now closes on the same note of triumph and assurance, as Paul drives home his point even more powerfully.

But can we really have genuine assurance? Before we further explore the confidence that God wants us to enjoy, it is worth pausing to acknowledge that in a postmodern world, any truth claims are deemed to be either fictitious or an abuse of power. We live in an age where it is deemed 'cool' and/or 'authentic' to doubt our ability to have confidence and assurance about anything or anyone.

The thing about this 'humble agnostic' position, however, is that it's not so humble. The agnostic not only claims that they can't know anything for certain, but often they confidently assert that no-one else can either. Their claims about the lack of absolute truth end up taking the form of an absolute truth claim.

By the time most students complete their first-year university studies in either philosophy or English literature, their confidence in their ability to know an author's intention has been all but eroded. This is more than a little ironic, given that the same lecturers who sabotage that confidence get very upset about being misunderstood when their own books are unfairly reviewed. They expect their readers to understand them, even while they're in the middle of claiming that no reader can really understand an author!

Theologian Don Carson makes a lot of sense when he responds to the perpetual skepticism of the postmodern world by affirming that while it is true that we do not know things exhaustively, we may know them truly.[80] "[Human beings] may approach greater and more accurate knowledge," he writes, "even though they can never gain absolute knowledge".

Experience tells me that I can know my wife truly, even though I don't know her exhaustively. There are many mysteries yet to explore and many depths to plumb. We wouldn't get out of bed if we really believed we could have no true knowledge about the world. We certainly wouldn't drive on the road if we didn't believe that every driver could read the road signs with a common mind and understand their meaning.

Jesus certainly assumed that he could and would be understood. While Pilate hid behind the cowardly agnostic position, "What is truth?" (John 18:38), Jesus expressed no doubt that he is "the truth", claiming that "the reason I was born and came into the world is to testify to the truth. Everyone on the side of truth listens to me" (John 18:37). Jesus quoted the Scriptures as if they can be both understood and relied upon (even though the copies of the Old

---

80 DA Carson, 'Systematic Theology and Biblical Theology', in *New Dictionary of Biblical Theology*, TD Alexander and Brian S Rosner (eds), IVP, Downers Grove, 2000, p. 100.

Testament Scriptures to which he had access would not have been the original manuscripts, but were the result of generations of faithful copying). His language is consistent with God's sovereign authority in his word, captured in Isaiah 55: "…so is my word that goes out from my mouth: It will not return to me empty, but will accomplish what I desire and achieve the purpose for which I sent it" (v. 11)

In short, God speaks expecting to be understood. He is in total control of his original spoken words in history, of the process of the faithful recording of those words for subsequent generations, and of our understanding and comprehension of his word (e.g. Matt 22:29; John 10:27; Rom 3:2).

In the face of so many challenges from Satan, from sin, from suffering, and from self-recrimination, what level of confidence does God's word offer to us? Is assurance *really* possible? And more specifically, what is our response to God's sovereign and electing grace, which locates our suffering within God's eternal plan?

The final section of Romans 8 celebrates the assurance that is ours, and it does so by daring anyone to deny our place in God's plan. Paul throws out question after question to show that the truth and the depth of God's love for us cannot be refuted. He anticipates accusations that cannot be upheld. Here are the questions that Paul uses to highlight five irrefutable truths (vv. 31-36).

Q1. "If God is for us, who can be against us?" (v. 31)
In one sense, the answer is "Nobody". But in another sense, perhaps the more accurate answer is "Everybody, but who cares?!"

With God on your side, you will ultimately never come off

second-best. Once you have worked out that there is no-one more powerful than the sole Creator and Sustainer of the universe, once you have concluded that nothing and no-one can thwart, frustrate or hinder God's purposes, then you know that victory is always assured.

We are tempted to misread painful situations as if God were against us, or to see suffering as evidence that God does not have our back. We wrongly conclude that God either hates us or doesn't seek our good. We fear that our failures become opportunities for God to turn on us, either now or in the future. But God has already shown us that he is always, always *for* us. Whenever you are tempted to doubt this fact, go back to the cross. The cross is the indisputable evidence that God is utterly for us—as Paul goes on to show.

Q2. "He who did not spare his own Son, but gave him up for us all—how will he not also, along with him, graciously give us all things?" (v. 32)
Paul uses a common rhetorical technique: the shift from the greater to the lesser, or from the harder to the easier. This is not unlike the "how much more" argument of Romans 5:9-10: to paraphrase, "If Christ died for us while we were enemies, *how much more* will he save us now that we are friends!" In other words, if God has done the greatest, hardest thing of all, it's guaranteed that he will also do the lesser, easier thing. The hardest thing God ever had to do was to sacrifice his own Son for us all. God did what he would ultimately not allow Abraham to do (Genesis 22).

If that is the case, how is it possible to think that God will hold back on giving you the rest of what he promised? If he didn't withhold his own Son, do you think he will withhold:

- your resurrected body?
- your declaration of total forgiveness?
- your adoption as a child of God?
- your place in the new creation?
- your eternal life?
- [anything that is genuinely in your best interests as you live this life?]

In one sense, I am all for the prosperity gospel, which promises God's people health and wealth. It's just a matter of getting the timing right. God *will* graciously give us all things—but we will only fully experience that in the age to come. To promise heaven on earth in this age is just plain cruel. And yet failure to help people understand what God actually does promise is no less cruel.

Perhaps you think you have disqualified yourself from being able to trust God at this point. Are there sins still lurking; is there guilt still condemning? Is Satan still accusing? Are you tempted to doubt that God will graciously give you all things?

With that possibility in mind, let us turn to question 3.

Q3. "Who will bring any charge against those whom God has chosen? It is God who justifies." (v. 33)

The early chapters of Romans depict a courtroom scene. In Romans 1:18-3:20, God effectively tells everybody, Jew and Gentile, to "Shut up!" God declares that no-one is righteous—not even one—and that all people everywhere are under the power of sin (Rom 3:19-20). On our own, we all stand condemned with no defence to offer.

But for those who have put their trust in Jesus, God will

not allow us to remain condemned. We have been justified. God declares us "Not guilty". There is now no accusation to be made against those in Christ Jesus.

Let me repeat myself. You can know now what God is going to say about you on the last day, and that verdict is an emphatic, loud and clear, "Not guilty!" Those God personally chose are those God is entitled to justify.

So who will be able to stand now, or on the last day, and deny what God has already pronounced over you? Satan may try, but he is not entitled to bring any charge. Even though his name means 'accuser', he has been disarmed at the cross (Col 2:15). He is like one of those gummy sharks I once caught on the North Coast of NSW. They are impressive and they might seem scary, but they have absolutely no teeth. Since Satan can't condemn you on the Day of Judgement, don't let him do it now. To change metaphors, Satan may shoot accusations your way, but you must remember that he is shooting blanks. In God's eyes, you are exactly as righteous as Christ himself!

Those who are not Christian are also denied the right to bring any charge against God's elect. When you fail, they may say, "I thought you were supposed to be a Christian". But on the last day, they will not be entitled to list your many sins. The accusations won't stick, for in Christ we are like Teflon when it comes to such charges. The price for our sins has already been paid at the cross!

It's not that we don't sin in the present age, and it's not as though it's okay for Christians to say one thing and do another. It's not as if we don't need to confess our sins to both God and to others. And yes, God is impacted by our disobedience. Our sins do grieve God's Spirit (Eph 4:30), and it is right to feel bad when we wound God. But it is absolutely critical to remember that we have a Spirit of sonship, not slavery. We have regrets, yes, but there is no condemnation for us.

We fear the Lord so that we can serve the Lord without fear (Luke 1:74; 1 John 4:18). For a believer, the fear of the Lord results in awe and worship and a trembling at God's word (Isa 66:5). For unbelievers, the fear of the Lord is the terror of a Christless eternity (Heb 10:31). Speaking of the appropriate fear of God experienced by believers, Ed Welch writes:

> But this [fear of terror] is only one end of the fear of the Lord. At the other end of the spectrum is a fear reserved exclusively for those who have put their faith in Jesus Christ. This fear of the Lord means reverent submission that leads to obedience, and it is interchangeable with "worship," "rely on," "trust," and "hope in." Like terror, it includes a knowledge of our sinfulness and God's moral purity, and it includes a clear-eyed knowledge of God's justice and His anger against sin. But this worship-fear also knows God's great forgiveness, mercy and love.[81]

We need to know that in Christ, we can't make God angry! He will discipline us as a Father lovingly disciplines his children (Heb 12:7-8), but his wrath was averted at the cross once and for all (John 3:36; Rom 3:25; 1 John 2:2).

We've mentioned Satan, and we've mentioned other people. But it's also worth saying that you are not entitled to

---

[81] Welch, *When People Are Big*, pp. 97-8.

bring any charge against yourself. Who do you think you are to bring a charge against the very one God chose before time began, even if the one you condemn is yourself?

I've often heard the words, "I know God forgives me, but I can't forgive myself". On the surface, those words have an air of humility, but in reality they betray a subtle form of pride. How could I allow my opinion of myself to outrank God's declaration, which is grounded in his loving election before time and in his Son's precious blood? What I think of myself must never be more important than what God thinks of me.

Part of our repentance is to think God's thoughts after him. To do anything less is to place ourselves on the throne of God. Imagine an accused man standing in the courtroom, having just been pronounced 'Not guilty' by the judge, telling the judge that he is wrong—refusing to receive the verdict and asking to be returned to prison. What kind of madness would that be?

You may need to give yourself a good talking-to by preaching the gospel of grace to the person whose face you see in the mirror each morning. There is only one rightful judge, and it's not you. And the one rightful judge has already promised that he will not condemn his own children.

I'm not denying the reality of our emotions, which can speak louder and feel more real than the text of Scripture. And for those with clinical depression and anxiety, please factor in the impact of your mental health. Don't underestimate the blessing of medication such as anti-depressants, which may allow you to engage in the battle for truth without having your hands tied behind your back. But the approach Paul takes here is one of defiance towards that part of us that wants to self-loathe and self-condemn.

Q4. "Who then is the one who condemns? No-one. Christ Jesus who died—more than that, who was raised to life—is at the right hand of God and is also interceding for us." (v. 34)

The only one who has the right to condemn is the judge. The only appointed judge of the universe is Christ Jesus (e.g. John 5:27; Acts 17:31). Now, is that same Christ going to condemn you? Let's remind ourselves again what he has already done, and what he is doing for you right now.

This is the same Christ who came in the likeness of sinful man and took those nails for you at the cross. Is that same Christ now going to take back the offer of forgiveness?

This is the same Christ who was delivered over to death for your sins and was raised to life for your justification. Is that same Christ going to now condemn you, after he has gone to such lengths to acquit you?

This is the same Christ who now is at the right hand of God. And what do you think Jesus is doing at the right hand of the Father? Is he blowing the whistle on you to the other persons of the Trinity? Is he slandering you before the heavenly host? Is he hurling one accusation after another against you to the Father?

Resist the urge to be paranoid. You'll never find Jesus talking behind your back to the Father with words like: "He is such a gutless, pathetic Christian, and I'm so fed up with him"; or "Forget her, Father. She still hasn't managed to regularly read her Bible and say her prayers after eight years of being a Christian, and then she belly aches that I seem far away"; or "Ditch him, Dad. I've had enough! Do you know he still watches pornography after claiming to be one with us? He is hopeless!"

Is that what Christ Jesus is doing at the right hand of the Father?

NO! NO! NO!

Jesus does not deny our guilt or make cheap excuses. But neither does he condemn us because of our failures.

So what is he doing? Every moment of every day, in the midst of every sin you commit, the Son is seated at God's right hand interceding *for you*, not against you. He is applying his death to your sins, declaring each one paid in full.

What kept Christ on the cross was not the nails, but his love. And that same love keeps Christ at the right hand of the Father. The ultimate ground of our assurance is the love of God in Christ.

No wedge can ever come between you and that love.

As he asks the last of his five questions, Paul now desperately scoops up any possible situation that might be thought of as denying Christ's love.

Q5. "Who shall separate us from the love of Christ? Shall trouble or hardship or persecution or famine or nakedness or danger or sword? As it is written: 'For your sake we face death all day long; we are considered as sheep to be slaughtered'." (vv. 35-36)

Where did we get the idea that coming to Christ meant no more pain? Where did we get the idea that if God's love is upon us, we will not suffer? This common misunderstanding is why Paul quotes Psalm 44, of all passages. In this psalm, God's people lament the fact that their enemies have crushed them, even though they had not forgotten God or been false to his covenant (Ps 44:17). Their suffering was not the result of their sin, nor was it a denial of God's unfailing love. And for God's people today, this kind of suffering is simply part and parcel of following a crucified, suffering Messiah and living in a fallen world.

But Paul is desperately keen for us to know that, even though this life will be painful and difficult, the sufferings of this life can't affect our eternal destiny. Michael Hutchence from INXS wanted to conquer the world, but that is far too small a goal for those of us who have been called by God. That just won't do. God wants us to be more than conquerors!

More than conquerors…

> No, in all these things we are more than conquerors through him who loved us. For I am convinced that neither death nor life, neither angels nor demons, neither the present nor the future, nor any powers, neither height nor depth, nor anything else in all creation, will be able to separate us from the love of God that is in Christ Jesus our Lord. (Rom 8:37-39)

If you want to conquer the world, don't let anything conquer your confidence in Christ's love. To bolster our confidence, Paul makes a list of the things that can't drive a wedge between Christ's love and us.

Neither death nor life

Elsewhere, Paul confidently asserts: "For to me, to live is Christ and to die is gain" (Phil 1:21). Die young or die old, either way we die in Christ. That is what we call a win-win scenario.

One of the great privileges of being at the bedside of a

believer who is about to die is to whisper the words of Jesus: "Today you will be with Jesus in paradise" (cf. Luke 23:43). Don't let your minister have all the joy. You are just as entitled to speak the same words of eternal life to anyone who is united to Christ.

Neither angels nor demons

As we have seen, Satan's mouth is silenced. You can call out to the demons of hell, "Which of you is going to condemn me?" and hell will freeze over before one of them will be allowed to accuse you and deny Christ's love. As one person told me, "Satan may know your past, but you know his future".

Neither the present nor the future

In a world with so much uncertainty, in Christ our future holds no surprises and the present holds no ultimate fears. It's not that we know everything that will happen, and not that our future in this life will be blissfully happy. But whatever the future holds, it can't hold a candle to what God has done for us in Christ. Neither can anything that happens in the present. It ultimately holds no fears for us.

Once the future is secure, we can live with confidence in the present, no matter what happens moment by moment. I have a strange habit of listening to my favourite rugby league team's results before I watch the game. Once I know we have won the game, it makes the 80-minute viewing experience so different. My team can play badly, and the opposing team can score lots of tries and be ahead for 79 minutes, and it still just doesn't bother me. Why? Because I know that in the 80th minute, my team will win. That is how the Christian life is lived. No matter what roller coasters of emotions or challenges we experience, the outcome is guaranteed. We live in light of the end.

Nor any powers, neither height nor depth, nor anything else in all creation
That pretty much covers everything and everyone, so be convinced!

It's worth recalling that this confidence comes from a man who designated himself as the 'worst of sinners' (1 Tim 1:15). He saw himself this way because of his violent opposition to the church of Christ, openly and honestly remembering how intensely he had "persecuted the church of God and tried to destroy it"(Gal 1:13; cf. Acts 8:1, 9:1-2). Saul was the fundamentalist terrorist of the first century, a man who wreaked havoc on any who were not ashamed of Christ. But this same Saul was converted after he was confronted by the living Lord Jesus on the road to Damascus. As part of his conversion, he was directed to take the good news of the resurrected Son of God to the nations.

Paul would later describe his new life in Christ this way: "The life I now live in the body, I live by faith in the Son of God, who loved me and gave himself for me" (Gal 2:20b). If anyone was legitimately tempted to have Satan condemn them for past sins, it was Paul. And if anyone had a sufficient quota of sufferings to think God may have hated them, it was Paul—a man who (somewhat ironically) was thrown in jail and whose very life was threatened once he started preaching Christ crucified. And yet, while he never forgot that he was the 'worst of sinners', and while his sufferings were very real, he knew nothing could separate him—or us—from the love of God in Christ Jesus.

Paul shares his confidence in Romans 8 not to gloat, but so that we all might share the same confidence as we grasp God's radical, loving commitment to his people through their Saviour. That is why Paul was not ashamed of the gospel (Rom 1:16), and why he wanted the Roman Christians not to be ashamed of the gospel: because through the gospel, we can have complete assurance of God's love for us in Christ Jesus. As a result, Paul's ambition was to preach the good news where Christ's love was not known (Rom 15:20). This was a love that needed to be enjoyed. This love needed to be celebrated, and it needed to be shared.

Keeping up appearances

Anonymous

I have become pretty good at pretending. To most people who know me, I live a fairly busy life. I'm a 'people person', often mistaken for an extrovert. I have fallen (or dug my way) into the category of the 'helper' and have settled nicely. It feels as though many think they know me well, but I feel as though only a very select few do, if that.

For the last three years, I have battled with depression. But I'll only ever tell people I'm feeling 'down' or 'flat', as if it sounds better. I find it embarrassing; it's something I've been ashamed of for years. As if it were a sin, or a dark secret you hide that keeps you up at night. I like the way people see me; I want them to think I'm capable, not in need of help or a 'night off' from serving at church. I'd rather tell them I had a good day instead of telling them I stayed in bed.

Busyness has become the perfect cover. When I am well, it means I finally have productive days and I'm able to play catch up. When I'm unwell, it means being unable to attend events is believable because, well, "You are always busy".

I feel weak. In that weakness, I play the comparison game. If only I was like my mum, I wouldn't be so 'emotional' and I would have a greater capacity to work, to serve. If only I was more like my dad, I could control my emotions better.

I should clarify that I am writing this in March 2017, and February was one of the lowest months I have experienced. Depression is still relatively new for me, though the last few years have felt very long. Growing up, depression was never something I faced. I was genuinely one of the happiest kids and even teenagers you could find. A few events in my final year of school made it a very painful year. After school, I went overseas and had an incredible, fruitful year. But upon coming back to Sydney, all the pain from that last year of school caught up with me. I found myself lost in my own city and with my closest friends having moved away and/or fallen away from God, I felt lost and isolated. This was the beginning of some very dark days.

The down times have come in seasons. I may have a few months of feeling great and healthy. Most often it comes every month or two, only for a few days. Like last month, however, there are occasions where the fog is constant, day in and day out. It can be so unrelenting and it feels as though it will never let up.

The practical implications of depression have had an impact on day-to-day living. I've had to take time off university, and try three different types of medications—only recently having changed again as I still haven't found what works. Then there are the side effects: dizziness, nausea, exhaustion, and poor sleep. Bailing on friends and family last minute. Not being able to live my life as fast-paced as I'd like.

The greatest struggle when it comes to my relationship with God is having faith. You see, depression isn't what I feel; it is what I think. Obviously it is what I end up feeling, but those feelings are rooted in the firm and unrelenting thoughts I have of myself. On the other side, I was always taught that my walk with God was to not be dependent on my feelings, but upon the truth of the gospel. And that is not something that can be swayed. I do not need to 'feel' the presence of God in order to know he is there. But now I am convinced of two ways of thinking: the gospel of our Lord Jesus Christ, and my depression; and they could not contradict each other more.

This illness makes me question everything. Does my family love me? Do my friends care, or are they just being polite? Are people at church nice to me because I'm a deacon's kid? People at work probably only like me because I smile and don't have a downturned mouth.

I enjoy a good laugh, and even more so I love to make people laugh. But there is something uniquely painful about making others laugh when you fear that your days will be marked with sadness.

Recently I have been dwelling on the verse where Jesus says 'deny yourself and take up your cross' (Mark 8:34). I understand the context of the passage, but I see it as applicable to this. To deny oneself is to deny your desires, thoughts and actions. For me, that means denying my thoughts, denying the way I see myself, and seeing myself through the lens of the cross of Christ.

"Who will bring any charge against those whom God has chosen?… Who then is the one who condemns?" No-one!

"For I am convinced that neither death nor life, neither angels nor demons, neither the present nor the future, nor any powers, neither height nor depth, nor anything else in all creation, will be able to separate us from the love of God that is in Christ Jesus our Lord."

Not only will my darkest thoughts not separate me from the love of God, but I don't have the right to condemn myself. Now, I wouldn't go around saying that to someone who is depressed, but it is worth pondering: why do we think others can't judge us, but we think we can judge ourselves rather than letting God's word speak truth into our lives?

But if I was to be honest with you, I struggle to have Paul's confidence. The confidence we have as Christians in this lifetime is a gift, and yet it's as though this gift is for those without mental illness. The reality is that when the fog sets in, I won't feel this confidence.

Whether I 'feel' the words Paul is preaching or not, I can see the importance of preaching them to myself, even while there will be days and perhaps seasons in which I won't 'feel' them to be true. I will either be feeding my mind the truths of the gospel or I will be feeding my mind the lies of my depression. I say this to you on a better day, knowing that it will seem almost impossible to believe these things on a bad day.

Please pray that I deny my negative thoughts and submit myself to Jesus Christ, knowing that it is he alone that can satisfy me. Pray that I would live my life reflecting this truth.

Conclusion

In my office, above my desk, is a print of a well-known photograph by Jean Guichard.[82] The photo shows a 47-metre high lighthouse called La Jument, which stands off the coast of France, being thrashed by 10-metre waves.

The first time this photo caught my eye, I was impressed because there is something attractive about the sheer resistance of the lighthouse, its impenetrable structure able to withstand the force of the powerful waves. Regardless of the pounding of the sea, the lighthouse remains immovable. Here is something we all wish we could be—confidently standing true, no matter what struggles and sufferings wash over us. But that is not why I wanted a copy of the photo.

As you look more closely at the lighthouse, you notice the tiny figure of a man standing in the doorway. You barely notice him at first. When I saw him, I said to myself, "You idiot, Ray. You are not the lighthouse. You're the man hiding in the safety of this immovable construction." If the lighthouse represents anyone, it represents God and his invincible

---

82 You can see the photograph here: www.jean-guichard.com/photos/france/brittany-finistere/ouessant/la-jument-00011.

purposes. But that is still not why I wanted a copy of the photo.

I wanted the photo because I noticed that the man had one of his hands in his pocket. It's the stance of a man in a relaxed state. He knew those massive waves were not going to harm him, because that lighthouse was not going to budge. Similarly, the invincible purposes of God will allow neither sin nor suffering to cast us adrift from his love in Christ Jesus.

It's time that those of us who are in Christ put our hands in our pockets and relaxed, secure in the confidence that God will have his way. If God is for us, who can be against us?

> For I am convinced that neither death nor life, neither angels nor demons, neither the present nor the future, nor any powers, neither height nor depth, nor anything else in all creation, will be able to separate us from the love of God that is in Christ Jesus our Lord. (Rom 8:38-39)

God not only wants to save you. He wants you to know that you are saved. And he wants that knowledge to transform your life.

Postscript

If you know the story of the photo, you may be aware that the tiny figure, Théodore Malgorn, opened the door of the lighthouse to see the helicopter just as Guichard was taking the shot. Suddenly realizing that a giant wave was about to engulf the structure, Théodore rushed back inside just in time to save his life.

Perhaps this is closer to the real story of the Christian life and the key to Romans 8.

In Christ, we are both relaxed and forever rushing into the safe arms of the loving Father, the faithful Son, and the powerful Holy Spirit. We live this way as we are pounded by the inevitable waves of sin and suffering, as we live between here and eternity.

Acknowledgements

Writing this book was like giving birth to an elephant. At times I was not sure whether it was going to see the light of day. It's been written by the grace of God and with the help of so many people. I thank God for the Katoomba Christian Convention, and for the privilege they gave by inviting me to preach on this most beautiful passage in the mid-1990s. A very special thanks to Geoff Robson for his insightful editorial work and his kind words in the foreword. As always, I am indebted to my wife, Sandy, and my church, MBM Rooty Hill Anglican. They are both a constant and amazing encouragement to my soul.

A big thanks to the army of helpers who, in different ways, helped to make this book possible. These include Jo Bailey, Phil and Anne Gilchrist, Ed Johnson, Malcolm Gill, Brandon Bonnici, Matt Olliffe, Geoff Lindsay, Fiona Hingston, Madeleine Galea, Bruce and Cathey Clarke, the Evans family, the hospitality of St Matthew's Anglican Church Manly, Emma Thornett, and Tony Payne.

I am particularly grateful for the contributors to this book, who told their honest, painful and uplifting stories, and in so doing put flesh on Romans 8. These include Paul

Grimmond, Grant Dibden, Wendy and Shaun Potts, Steve Jeffrey, Julie Lamplough and Phillip Jensen.

Appendices

A
Romans 8

¹ Therefore, there is now no condemnation for those who are in Christ Jesus, ² because through Christ Jesus the law of the Spirit who gives life has set you free from the law of sin and death. ³ For what the law was powerless to do because it was weakened by the flesh, God did by sending his own Son in the likeness of sinful flesh to be a sin offering. And so he condemned sin in the flesh, ⁴ in order that the righteous requirement of the law might be fully met in us, who do not live according to the flesh but according to the Spirit.

⁵ Those who live according to the flesh have their minds set on what the flesh desires; but those who live in accordance with the Spirit have their minds set on what the Spirit desires. ⁶ The mind governed by the flesh is death, but the mind governed by the Spirit is life and peace. ⁷ The mind governed by the flesh is hostile to God; it does not submit to God's law, nor can it do so. ⁸ Those who are in the realm of the flesh cannot please God.

⁹ You, however, are not in the realm of the flesh but are in the realm of the Spirit, if indeed the Spirit of God lives in you. And if anyone does not have the Spirit of Christ, they do not belong to Christ. ¹⁰ But if Christ is in you, then even though your body is subject to death because of sin, the Spirit gives life because of righteousness. ¹¹ And if the Spirit of him who raised Jesus from the dead is living in you, he who raised Christ from the dead will also give life to your mortal bodies because of his Spirit who lives in you.

¹² Therefore, brothers and sisters, we have an obligation—but it is not to the flesh, to live according to it. ¹³ For if you live according to the flesh, you will die; but if by the Spirit you put to death the misdeeds of the body, you will live.

¹⁴ For those who are led by the Spirit of God are the children of God. ¹⁵ The Spirit you received does not make you slaves, so that you live in fear again; rather, the Spirit you received brought about your adoption to sonship. And by him we cry, "Abba, Father." ¹⁶ The Spirit himself testifies with our spirit that we are God's children. ¹⁷ Now if we are children, then we are heirs—heirs of God and co-heirs with Christ, if indeed we share in his sufferings in order that we may also share in his glory.

¹⁸ I consider that our present sufferings are not worth comparing with the glory that will be revealed in us. ¹⁹ For the creation waits in eager expectation for the children of God to be revealed. ²⁰ For the creation was subjected to frustration, not by its own choice, but by the will of the one who subjected it, in hope ²¹ that the creation itself will be liberated from its bondage to decay and brought into the freedom and glory of the children of God.

²² We know that the whole creation has been groaning

as in the pains of childbirth right up to the present time. ²³ Not only so, but we ourselves, who have the firstfruits of the Spirit, groan inwardly as we wait eagerly for our adoption to sonship, the redemption of our bodies. ²⁴ For in this hope we were saved. But hope that is seen is no hope at all. Who hopes for what they already have? ²⁵ But if we hope for what we do not yet have, we wait for it patiently.

²⁶ In the same way, the Spirit helps us in our weakness. We do not know what we ought to pray for, but the Spirit himself intercedes for us through wordless groans. ²⁷ And he who searches our hearts knows the mind of the Spirit, because the Spirit intercedes for God's people in accordance with the will of God.

²⁸ And we know that in all things God works for the good of those who love him, who have been called according to his purpose. ²⁹ For those God foreknew he also predestined to be conformed to the image of his Son, that he might be the firstborn among many brothers and sisters. ³⁰ And those he predestined, he also called; those he called, he also justified; those he justified, he also glorified.

³¹ What, then, shall we say in response to these things? If God is for us, who can be against us? ³² He who did not spare his own Son, but gave him up for us all—how will he not also, along with him, graciously give us all things? ³³ Who will bring any charge against those whom God has chosen? It is God who justifies. ³⁴ Who then is the one who condemns? No-one. Christ Jesus who died—more than that, who was raised to life—is at the right hand of God and is also interceding for us. ³⁵ Who shall separate us from the love of Christ? Shall trouble or hardship or persecution or famine or nakedness or danger or sword? ³⁶ As it is written:

> "For your sake we face death all day long;
> we are considered as sheep to be slaughtered."

37 No, in all these things we are more than conquerors through him who loved us. 38 For I am convinced that neither death nor life, neither angels nor demons, neither the present nor the future, nor any powers, 39 neither height nor depth, nor anything else in all creation, will be able to separate us from the love of God that is in Christ Jesus our Lord.

B
Setting the scene: Romans 1-7

The writer of this letter is none other than a former killer of Christians and the self-proclaimed 'worst of sinners' (1 Tim 1:15). But everything changed when the resurrected Lord Jesus confronted Paul (or Saul, as he was also known) in the original 'Damascus Road experience'. The ascended Lord Jesus not only commanded Paul to repent; he also gave Paul specific orders to take the radical message of grace to the nations (Acts 9:15).

Roman citizens were expected to declare that 'Caesar is Lord'. But Paul opens his letter to Christians living in Rome, at the heart of the empire, by declaring that Jesus Christ is Lord (Rom 1:4). At the heart of Christianity's subversive good news is that Christ alone, not Caesar, is the ultimate Emperor, both in this age and the age to come.

Thus Paul begins this majestic letter by defining his gospel, the gospel concerning Jesus:

- It is God's message concerning his Son, the long-awaited son of David (the Messiah) as foretold in the Scriptures (1:3; cf. 2 Samuel 7). Jesus didn't appear on the stage of history unannounced or in a vacuum.
- The gospel concerns Jesus' death-destroying resurrection, which ushers in the age of the Spirit (1:4).
- The gospel results in "the obedience that comes from faith", literally "the obedience of faith" (1:5). It was a transformational message, not simply information.
- This message is an international gospel for all nations (1:5-6), hence Paul's desire to use Rome as a launch pad to take the gospel to Spain and preach on a virgin canvas (cf. 15:24-28).
- The gospel will provide the framework to address the Jew-Gentile tensions that marked most New Testament churches, including the church in Rome.

It was critical that the Christians in Rome were on the same gospel page, given that Paul had not been there before. As a result, it's in this letter that the apostle gives the clearest and most profound explanation of both the gospel and the call to live a life worthy of the gospel. And Paul unashamedly affirms that this gospel is powerful to save anyone who trusts the promises concerning Christ—regardless of what they have done (apart from the law) or where they come from (Jew or Gentile; 1:16).

To properly grasp the good news, however, it is necessary to first face the bad news.

In 1:18-32, the righteousness of God that saves also results in God's wrath being unleashed on human rebellion. The focus is on the nations, which are viewed as being "without excuse" because God has revealed his existence, his power, his moral expectations, and even the penalty for breaking his will. All people everywhere have "exchanged the truth about God for a lie", preferring to worship mere created things rather than the living and true God. As a result, God's present punishment is expressed in handing humans over to do what they want. What we call freedom, God calls punishment—our enslavement to sin.

Romans 2 shows that it's not as if the Jews (God's original chosen people) are exempt from God's wrath. While they have a unique place within God's plan of salvation, they fail to live up to what they know and what they teach. They may have first access to the privileges and oracles of God, but they are also the first in line for judgement.

The bottom line is that "Jews and Gentiles alike are all under the power of sin" (3:9), and "fall short of the glory of God" (3:23). There are absolutely no favourites and no exceptions.

So as we come to Romans 3:21-31, a critical issue faces us: How can God be right *and* declare us right when we are so clearly in the wrong? In other words, how can God be just *and* acquit humanity's guilt? The tension is resolved by the provision of Christ's substitutionary death on behalf of all those who believe.

Like a lightning rod, Christ on the cross deflects God's righteous anger away from us who deserve it (propitiation/atonement), and in so doing he sets us free (redemption) from a guilty verdict (justification), turning the day of wrath into the day of salvation (3:21-26). Christ's death changes *everything*. And because Christ has accomplished everything needed for our salvation, it's clear that there are no grounds for human boasting before God (3:27-31).

To demonstrate that point, in chapter 4 Paul turns to the Old Testament. Whether one lives 2000 years before Christ (like Abraham), 1000 years before Christ (like King David), or 2000 years after Christ (like us), the principle is exactly the same: a person is "justified by faith apart from works of the law" (3:28). Abraham is the model of faith: he "believed God, and it was credited to him as righteousness" (4:3; cf. Gen 15:6). This happened prior to Abraham's circumcision. He was counted as righteous not because of his own works, but simply because he trusted the promises of God.

In Romans 5:1-11, Paul outlines the benefits of justification by faith. These include the possibility of joy even in the face of suffering, which flows from the knowledge that "we have peace with God through our Lord Jesus Christ" (5:1). In Christ, the war between God and us is over. God brings the war to an end—not by destroying his enemies, but by making them his friends. God's love was displayed at the cross, where he gave us his best even when we were at our worst. That love is applied to us and made real in our hearts by the gift of the Spirit.

In Romans 5:12-21, Paul retells the story of salvation history on a larger canvas. There have only ever been two people who made a difference in the world; the rest of us are just footnotes. The first person was Adam, and the second is Christ. As humanity's head and representative, through his disobedience Adam essentially sold every image-bearer into slavery to sin and death. But by the obedience of Christ, the damage is more than reversed, as all those 'in Christ' are declared righteous.

In Romans 6, Paul delivers the call to live a life that is

consistent with the gospel and urges Christians to grasp that, since we have died with Christ, sin should no longer rule in our mortal bodies. Our union with Adam has been broken, meaning we are no longer "slaves to sin" (6:6, 16, 17, 20). When we died with Christ, we were not only freed from the punishment of sin; we were also freed from the controlling power of sin.

Our newfound union with Christ (cf. 6:3, 11, 23) means that the destiny of every believer is bound up with the destiny of Christ himself. So when they crucified Jesus, it's as though we were crucified. When he died, we died. When they buried him, they buried us. In Christ, we are now no longer under the jurisdiction of sin and death. We live in a new realm, united with a living Lord who has made us alive. We have a new master, and his name is Christ. To return to a life of sin is like the slave whose freedom was purchased at a great price, but who returns back to an old master who previously oppressed them.

Romans 7 has a special eye to Christians from a Jewish background. Paul has declared that our union with Christ means we have not only died to sin; we have also died to the law. We have not only been set free from sin; we have been set free from the law. For those in Rome who may be suspicious that Paul views the law as somehow sinful in itself, Romans 7 explores the nature of the Christian's relationship with the law.

In Romans 8:3-4, Paul will explain that what the law could not do, God did by sending his Son and his Spirit. In that context, Romans 7 is an elaboration on what the law could not do and why it could not do it. Paul is emphatic in insisting that the law is holy, righteous and good. However, the problem is with sin and the flesh, which exploits God's good law and incites more sin. As a result, this dynamic exposes the sinfulness of sin and in so doing shows that the law is in fact good but is unable to produce fruit on its own. Romans 7:5 summarizes the core issues around the law's inability to do what only God could do: "For when we were in the realm of the flesh, the sinful passions aroused by the law were at work in us, so that we bore fruit for death".

Most readers will be aware of the key question around how to interpret this chapter: Is Paul speaking of the experience of the Christian, or of the non-Christian? If Paul is speaking as a non-Christian, then how can he say, "I delight in God's law" (7:22a) and "Thanks be to God, who delivers me through Jesus Christ our Lord!" (7:25)? But equally, if Paul is speaking as a Christian, then how can he say, "I am unspiritual, sold as a slave to sin" (7:14b; cf. 7:24-25a)?

Significantly, Paul continually expresses this battle in the present tense in verses 14-25, which seems to indicate the state of a frustrated believer: "I do not understand what I do. For what I want to do I do not do, but what I hate I do" (7:15; cf. Gal 5:17). And verse 21 provides an important insight into this tension: "Although I want to do good, evil is right there with me". It seems there are two aspects to Paul. On the one hand, Paul has the desire to do good and he hates what is evil, which is a testimony to his union with Christ and to the work of the Spirit (cf. 12:9). However, Paul also experiences the frustrating inability to obey, which is the result of internalized evil (sin and the flesh) that has a real and ongoing influence on the saints. Hence the 'split', or the overlapping aspect of Paul's usage of the first person pronoun 'I'.

But the broader point throughout this section is about sin

and the flesh: the law is not the problem; sin and flesh is the problem. Chapter 7 offers a universal formula:

Law + flesh = more sin + death

We need Christ's sin-bearing death, which results in no condemnation, and the power and presence of the Spirit to enable us to bear fruit (7:6; 8:3-4). We are 'prisoners of sin' to the extent that the battle to put sin to death will continue in this age, but not in the sense that we are always powerless to produce fruit. That is, chapter 7 speaks to the realism of the Christian struggle, while chapter 8 speaks to why we can embrace that struggle with optimism in the work of Christ and in the presence, power, and privileges of the Spirit.

And so with the exasperation of the believer in mind, Paul asks God to set him free: "What a wretched man I am! Who will rescue me from this body that is subject to death? Thanks be to God, who delivers me through Jesus Christ our Lord!" (7:24-25a). The answer to that prayer is found in one of the most stunning chapters in the whole Bible—a chapter that starts with the confident declaration: "Therefore, there is now no condemnation for those who are in Christ Jesus" (8:1).

C
On predestination

*H*istorically, there have been a number of challenges to what is called the Reformed view of predestination, a view to which I hold. Because predestination is such an important theme in Romans 8 (and even more so in Romans 9), it's worth outlining some of those challenges, along with my responses.

Predestination refers to God's choice for a particular ministry role, not for salvation. So God chooses Paul and the Twelve to be apostles, and he chooses Israel to be a light to the nations.

It is true that God chooses people for certain roles. However, Romans 9 addresses the salvation of the Jews, many of whom had rejected the long-awaited Messiah. This same chapter begins with Paul's willingness to be cursed for the sake of Israel, if that were possible. Predestination clearly refers to salvation, not just ministry roles.

Predestination refers to God choosing people for the purpose of sanctification (to be holy and blameless), not for salvation.
The context of Romans 8:28-29 sees the goal of predestination as being our justification and glorification. While being more like Christ is a central theme in Roman 8:28, it's located within the broader plan of salvation. Interestingly, sanctification is not one of the five words used in the 'golden chain' of verses 28-29.

Predestination refers to God's choice on the basis of some future response on the part of the recipient. That is, God chooses them because he knows they will choose him.
The grounds for election—whether Israel's (Deut 9:4) or ours as new covenant believers—are never our response or the worthiness of the recipient (Rom 9:16). So, speaking of God's choice of Jacob (the younger brother) over Esau (the older brother), Paul affirms that this took place "in order that God's purpose in election might stand: not by works but by him who calls" (Rom 9:11b-12a).

Hence, God's sovereign grace in election reinforces the utterly undeserved nature of our salvation, for even faith and repentance are gifts from God (cf. Eph 2:8; 2 Tim 2:25).

Predestination is a corporate concept, not an individual idea. Hence it refers to chosen Israel, or those collectively in Christ, or the church of Christ. An individual becomes part of that elect group freely and willingly, via faith.
The questions raised about unfairness in Romans 9:14 and 9:19 make no sense if Paul is only dealing with corporate

concepts. There is nothing that can be described as 'unfair' if people simply choose to be part of God's elect church. That is, these questions themselves testify to the seemingly offensive nature of Paul's view of God's sovereignty in individual and personal election. And the comfort of Romans 8:31-36 is rendered empty if the ones whom God chooses are, in fact, simply those who choose God.

Predestination reflects the theology of Paul, not Jesus.
Jesus may not have used the word 'predestined', but he repeatedly teaches the concept. See, for example, Matthew 11:25-26; John 1:13; 6:37, 44; 10:26, 29.

Predestination as described here can't be right, as it violates God's just and loving character.
There are several problems with this argument. Firstly, you could say the same for any of God's judgements in the Bible, especially hell itself. Such arguments tend to use one doctrine against another, and one verse against another. In reality, we need to hold to all that God has said, not just some of it.

Secondly, we need to be more nuanced when it comes to understanding the love of God in Scripture. Don Carson rightly notices that God's love is used in five different ways in the Bible.[83] It simply will not do to reduce God's love to one concept.

---

83   DA Carson, *The Difficult Doctrine of the Love of God*, IVP, Leicester, 2000, pp. 17-21. The five ways that Carson identifies are: (1) The peculiar love of the Father for the Son, and of the Son for the Father; (2) God's providential love over all that he has made; (3) God's salvific stance toward his fallen world; (4) God's particular, selecting, effective love toward his elect; (5) God's love is sometimes said to be directed toward his own people in a provisional or conditional way—conditional, that is, on obedience.

Thirdly, it's worth noting that before Paul outlines God's electing love in Romans 8 and 9, he has already taken us to the cross, where God has demonstrated his justice (3:25-26) and his love (5:8-10). While I may feel that God's selective love in election is unfair, I am told to look to the cross, where God could not demonstrate more clearly that he is the definition of both love and justice.

Concerning predestination, Luther warns of the importance of approaching this subject through the lens of the cross:

> But do you follow the order of this Epistle [Romans]? Worry first about Christ and the Gospel, that you may recognize your sin and His grace; then fight your sin, as the first eight chapters here have taught; then, when you have reached the eighth chapter, and are under the cross and suffering, that will teach you the right doctrine of predestination, in the ninth, tenth, and eleventh chapters, and how comforting it is. For in the absence of suffering and the cross and the danger of death, one cannot deal with predestination without harm and without secret wrath against God.[84]

---

84 Martin Luther, *Commentary on Romans*, trans J Theodore Mueller, Zondervan, Grand Rapids, 1954, p. xxiv.

Common misconceptions on predestination, and responses from Romans

If God predestines, I don't have to worry about the lost.
"I have great sorrow and unceasing anguish in my heart. For I could wish that I myself were cursed and cut off from Christ for the sake of my people, those of my own race, the people of Israel." (9:2-4)

If God predestines, I don't have to evangelize because all God's elect will be saved anyway.
"How, then, can they call on the one they have not believed in? And how can they believe in the one of whom they have not heard? And how can they hear without someone preaching to them? And how can they preach unless they are sent? As it is written, 'How beautiful are the feet of those who bring good news!'" (10:14-15)

If God predestines, how can he blame us for our response to him?
"One of you will say to me: 'Then why does God still blame us? For who is able to resist his will?' But who are you, a human being, to talk back to God? 'Shall what is formed say to the one who formed it, "Why did you make me like this?"' Does not the potter have the right to make out of the same lump of clay some pottery for special purposes and some for common use?" (9:19-21)

If God predestines, I don't have to pray because it makes no difference.
"Brothers and sisters, my heart's desire and *prayer* to God for the Israelites is that they may be saved." (10:1)

If God predestines, I can remain ignorant or proud.
"I do not want you to be ignorant of this mystery, brothers and sisters, so that you may not be conceited: Israel has experienced a hardening in part until the full number of the Gentiles has come in…" (11:25)

If God predestines, then he is unfair.
"What then shall we say? Is God unjust? Not at all! For he says to Moses,

> 'I will have mercy on whom I have mercy,
>   and I will have compassion on whom I have
>   compassion.'" (9:14-15)

If God predestines, then people are in hell because they are not chosen.
"For we have already made the charge that Jews and Gentiles alike are all under the power of sin. As it is written:

> 'There is no-one righteous, not even one;
>   there is no-one who understands;
>   there is no-one who seeks God.
> All have turned away,
>   they have together become worthless;
> there is no-one who does good,
>   not even one…'

"There is no difference between Jew and Gentile, for all have sinned and fall short of the glory of God…" (3:9b-12, 22b-23)

Romans 8 in 44 key ideas

Romans 8 is one of the great chapters of the Bible, but also one of the most condensed chapters. It's jam-packed with ideas. For those of us who like short, sharp points, here are 44 key ideas from Romans 8:

1. God not only wants to save his people; he wants them to know they are saved. There is no condemnation.

2. You need the law of God to tell you what is right and wrong.

3. The law of God can't save you, and on its own it cannot motivate your obedience.

4. The Spirit of God is a person. The Spirit is a 'he', not an 'it'.

5. Jesus died for us so that we would obey him, not just enjoy his forgiveness.

6. You are by nature worse than you can think.

7. God's work in your life is more powerful than you imagine.
8. You should have a God-given optimism about your progress in the Spirit. You can change!
9. If God were to withdraw his Spirit, you would not and could not please God, nor could you obey him.
10. God does not expect that you will obey him without his involvement. You're empowered by the Spirit.
11. God does not expect that he will sanctify you without your involvement. There is no 'let go and let God'.
12. Christians are committed assassins when it comes to sin in their life. Born-again believers have a newfound hate in their heart for sin.
13. Your nature determines your thinking, your thinking determines your behaviour, and your behaviour determines your destiny.
14. God expects there to be a constant battle in the Christian's life. Get used to it. You're in God's fight club.
15. God wants you to engage in the battle with sin without fear of punishment. Read this point again, because it's that important!
16. There is no promise of being sinless in this life. It's living in fairyland to think otherwise.
17. Giving up the battle with sin is not an option for the Christian. Get up now and get back into the ring! Fight on!

18. God the Spirit will raise you to life as certainly as he raised Jesus. Be assured.

19. You owe the Spirit big time. Let him live up to his name in your life. He is the *Holy* Spirit.

20. You can't have Jesus without having the Spirit. There is no Spiritless Christianity.

21. You can't have the Spirit without having Jesus. There is no true Christless spirituality.

22. The Spirit of Jesus enables you to call the judge of the earth 'Dad'.

23. Your experience of assurance is related to your praying to God as 'Dad'.

24. Abba is not just a Swedish pop group, but an Aramaic word for 'Dad'.

25. God's Spirit testifies to your spirit that you are a child of God.

26. God's Spirit does not testify to your spirit about whether someone else is a child of God.

27. If you don't suffer with Christ, you can forget about enjoying the glory. No pain, no gain!

28. You can't compare suffering you experience now with the great glory that will be revealed to you. They're not even in the same universe.

29. Creation groans, even if we leave it untouched.

30. Creation is waiting with eager anticipation for your resurrection as a child of God.

31. Having the Spirit gives you a holy discontent. You groan because you have the firstfruits of the Spirit. You want more of God.

32. God's Spirit groans to the Father for you when you have no idea what to pray. God will not abandon you in your pain. He has your back.

33. Proof that you believe in the new creation is that you patiently endure suffering as you eagerly await your adoption.

34. When it comes to every event in your life, whether good or bad, God is in the thick of it! He works "in *all things*".

35. The promise that God is working for our good "in all things" only applies to those who love him.

36. The 'good' that God is working out has to do with becoming more and more like Jesus. Holiness outranks happiness every time.

37. Jesus is our older brother, ushering in a new family of people who 'look' just like him. This is legitimate Christian cloning.

38. God hand-picks people from before time, and every single one of these people will be in glory. There is a zero dropout rate.

39. You can either complain about election or rejoice that God has chosen you in Christ Jesus. Thank you, thank you, thank you, Lord!

40. Give yourself a good talking-to: nothing and no-one can tear you from God's love in Christ Jesus.

41. God is for you, Jesus is for you, and the Spirit is for you. All for one and all for you.

42. If God has done the hardest thing for you (at the cross), he will certainly do everything else he promises.

43. Hell will freeze over before any of Satan's accusations against you will stick.

44. One more time: God not only wants to save you. He also wants you to know that you are saved. Be convinced!

On the death of a grandson
Phillip Jensen

This is the text of the sermon delivered at the Thanksgiving Service for Nathan Barry, Phillip's grandson, on 24 January 2017. Nathan passed away on 12 January, aged 16. The passage for the sermon was Romans 8:26-39. The sermon is reproduced here with kind permission from Phillip and from Nathan's parents. For more on Nathan's story, visit www.ournathanbarry.wordpress.com.

I'll tell you two things about Nathan that may surprise you. Firstly, Nathan was a sinner. Secondly, Nathan was certain of his salvation.

In many ways, Nathan was just one of us: living, eating, drinking, laughing and crying, just as we all are. There was nothing particularly unique about Nathan. He had no Olympic gold medals, and he didn't write a famous novel or a great opera. He didn't have a PhD at 15 or have a singing voice that cracked crystal. There was nothing that would make him stand out and be remembered by everybody—other than his very unusual cancer and his early death.

And yet, if you will pardon a grandfather saying so, his character, while not unique, was very impressive. Nathan wasn't perfect. He knew it, and he wanted me to tell you that he sinned, and he sinned often. But in facing death, he had a consistent confidence in God that was disarming. He didn't become self-absorbed. He continued to care for others and he stood out as different: as calm before the storm, as thoughtful when others were panicking, as kind when life seemed to be so cruel. He knew he was going to face his maker as a sinner in need of salvation, but as he wrestled with this, he searched the Scriptures and developed a great certainty about his eternity.

For Nathan's certainty of entering heaven wasn't just a wishful thinking for a better life, a fantasy, or a pipe dream. He had no time for pious platitudes. He was far too cynical and sceptical to believe everything he was told. He was a critical thinker who, over the year of his illness, developed a deeply reasoned understanding of God and his purposes. And he wanted me to explain this to you today.

The passage Nathan chose for us today is Romans 8, because he found it so helpful as he wrestled in his conscience preparing for his death, and as he suffered in pain and prepared for glory. It's the passage that will explain Nathan to us.

Romans 8 explains that the sufferings of this present time are not worth comparing with the glory that is to be revealed in us. To simplify things, I have three headings:

1. Suffering
2. Sovereignty
3. Certainty

1. Suffering

While our society tries to avoid thinking about suffering, and pretend that all is well in our wonderful world, the Bible is so much more realistic. It confronts and reminds us of—and explains for us—the suffering of this world; suffering that at times is so acute, we don't know what to pray for. We're in such weakness and pain, sorrow and anguish, that all we can do is groan and sigh—and, of course, cry: "The Spirit helps us in our weakness. We do not know what we ought to pray for, but the Spirit himself intercedes for us through wordless groans" (v. 26).

This past year has been like that, as we prayed for healing in the face of conflicting, and increasingly sad, news of the spread of tumours. It can feel like this today as we give joyful thanks to God for Nathan, and yet internally our hearts are breaking with sorrow as we grieve for what we've lost and can't retrieve. Yet note in that verse that we're not left alone in prayerless mumbling. For the Spirit of God turns our tears and sighs, our groans and heartaches, into prayers to our Father in heaven.

2. Sovereignty

As we come to God in prayer, we're reminded of what we know about our sovereign God: "And we know that in all things God works for the good of those who love him, who have been called according to his purpose" (v. 28).

God rules as the sovereign, as the king, as the ruler over all things, so that all things work together for God's good purpose in the lives of his children. There's nothing outside of his care or control. Nothing that happened to Nathan this last year was outside of God's control or God's concern. Neither Nathan nor God lost the battle against cancer. It was all part and parcel of God's good purpose for Nathan.

At first this sounds extraordinary—but God is God. He is sovereign. He doesn't lose control. And he has a good purpose for his children, explained in verse 29: "For those God foreknew he also predestined to be conformed to the image of his Son, that he might be the firstborn among many brothers and sisters".

What is God's good purpose for his children? What is the good life that we're destined to live? It's not a pain-free life in this world. The Bible is quite clear that in this world, man is born to trouble as surely as the sparks fly upwards. This last year of suffering has been awful. This last week of death has been dreadful. But God's plan for his children is to be conformed to the likeness of his glorious son, Jesus. That does not mean a pain-free life in this world; it means becoming like Jesus—the Suffering Servant, the Man of Sorrows, the crucified Christ. The man who bore all our sorrows and griefs. The man who laid down his life for others so that, in God's good time, we may become like him in glory, sharing his glory, and bringing him glory by being like him.

We see in verse 30 how God's sovereignty works out in our lives: "And those he predestined, he also called; those he called, he also justified; those he justified, he also glorified".

This passage is so confident of God's sovereignty in our salvation that it speaks of our salvation as a 'done deal': those whom he justified he also glorified.

3. Certainty

We know of the sufferings of this world. We know of the sovereignty of God over this world, using everything including our suffering to bring us to the glory we will share with Christ. Therefore, we know with certainty of our glorious future.

They say there are only two certainties about our future: death and taxes. Quite clearly, if you're rich enough, you can avoid taxes—so the only certainty is death. And death is so unpleasant and unknown that most people not only fight against it, but also go into denial—pretending, imagining that it's not going to happen or, worse, that it doesn't matter.

But once you know the sovereignty of God, working in all things for our glorification, then you have a certainty about the future, including death. That's what our passage is about, with its mounting tide of rhetorical questions in verses 31-36 and its magnificent affirmation of victory in verses 37-39. It's about our certainty.

The simple response to God's sovereign plan for our glory is the rhetorical challenge of verse 31: "If God is for us, who can be against us?" All the rest flows from the central challenge that though there are many things against us, none of them can stand against us if God is for us.

Do you think God is stingy? That he's going to go back on his promises? That he's not going to give us glory? Think again! He didn't spare his own Son in order to save us (v. 32). What do you think he is now going to deny us? If God is for us, who can be against us?

Do you think somebody will be able to point the finger at us, pointing out our sins and declaring us unfit for glory? Think again! It's God himself—the Judge of all the world—who has justified us by sending his Son to die for us (v. 33). If God is for us, who can be against us?

Do you think that somebody will be able to condemn us? Think again! "Christ Jesus who died—more than that, who was raised to life—is at the right hand of God and is also interceding for us" (v. 34). Jesus pleads our case for us. If God is for us, who can be against us?

Do you think that somebody or something could come between us and Christ's love for us? Think again! God loved us so much that he gave his Son for us (v. 32). His Son so loved us that he died for us. Suffering will not keep us from God in whatever form it comes: trouble, hardship, persecution, famine, nakedness, danger, or sword. Indeed, the Old Testament (quoted in verse 36) predicts our suffering as normal. But if God is for us, who can be against us?

So, our certainty rises to this magnificent affirmation of victory in verses 37-39:

> No, in all these things we are more than conquerors through him who loved us. For I am convinced that neither death nor life, neither angels nor demons, neither the present nor the future, nor any powers, neither height nor depth, nor anything else in all creation, will be able to separate us from the love of God that is in Christ Jesus our Lord.

Once you've grasped the love of God in Christ Jesus our Lord; once you've understood the sovereignty of God controlling all of your life (including your suffering and pain and cancer); once you've understood that this sovereign Lord loves you so much that he willingly laid down his life for you, paying for all your sin, enduring all your hell; once you have been grasped by the love of God in Christ Jesus our Lord; then you can look death in the face, with all its horror and anguish, and know: If God is for us, who can be against us?

Nathan knew this love of God in Christ Jesus, and as soon as he understood the gospel he wanted his friends and his family to be told about it. Nathan built his short life on this love of God in Christ Jesus. And so, when suffering came to him—in a way that nobody would have predicted, with a terrible terminus in death—he didn't change his direction; he didn't give up caring for others. While he hurt—and even the medicines given to him hurt—he still remained steadfast and confident in his suffering, knowing the sovereignty of God was at work in his glorification.

But he did take stock of his life. He knew he was a sinner, so he searched the Scriptures again to base his salvation in the certainty of God's word. And when he saw this passage in particular, he knew how his confidence was founded on the love of God in Christ Jesus. This is why today we don't so much honour Nathan, but we give thanks to God for him. This is why today we're not worried about Nathan's future, but we give thanks to God for his salvation. This is why today we can rejoice in our sorrow and praise God in Nathan's death.

But Nathan would be very disappointed in me, and in fact he would not so gently chide me, if I didn't also ask you whether you have this same certainty—whether you know this God who so loves his people. Whether you are hearing in the death of his servant Nathan the call to come to God.

Young man, young woman, do you hear the call of God? Listen and come to him. Parents, do you hear the call of God? Listen and come to him. Old man, old woman, do you hear the call of God? Listen and come to him. For rest assured that one day you too, like Nathan, will die. One day you too will meet your maker. And as a sinner like Nathan, what will you say on that day? What will be your response? What will you say in your defence? Who will intercede on your behalf?

I know Nathan's response: "Jesus Christ died for me". I know who intercedes on Nathan's behalf: Jesus Christ, who died for him and rose again to sit at God's right hand.

That is why, with sorrowful joy, we give thanks to God and sing his praises. For nothing will separate Nathan from the love of God in Christ Jesus his Lord.

Feedback on this resource

We really appreciate getting feedback about our resources—not just suggestions for how to improve them, but also positive feedback and ways they can be used. We especially love to hear that the resources may have helped someone in their Christian growth.

You can send feedback to us via the 'Feedback' menu in our online store, or write to us at info@matthiasmedia.com.au.

Matthias Media is an evangelical publishing ministry that seeks to persuade all Christians of the truth of God's purposes in Jesus Christ as revealed in the Bible, and equip them with high-quality resources, so that by the work of the Holy Spirit they will:

- abandon their lives to the honour and service of Christ in daily holiness and decision-making
- pray constantly in Christ's name for the fruitfulness and growth of his gospel
- speak the Bible's life-changing word whenever and however they can—in the home, in the world and in the fellowship of his people.

Our resources range from Bible studies and books through to training courses, audio sermons and children's Sunday School material. To find out more, and to access samples and free downloads, visit our website:

www.matthiasmedia.com

How to buy our resources

1. Direct from us over the internet:
   – in the US: www.matthiasmedia.com
   – in Australia: www.matthiasmedia.com.au

2. Direct from us by phone: please visit our website for current phone contact information.

3. Through a range of outlets in various parts of the world. Visit **www.matthiasmedia.com/contact** for details about recommended retailers in your part of the world.

4. Trade enquiries can be addressed to:
   – in the US and Canada: sales@matthiasmedia.com
   – in Australia and the rest of the world: sales@matthiasmedia.com.au

---

Register at our website for our **free** regular email update to receive information about the latest new resources, **exclusive special offers**, and free articles to help you grow in your Christian life and ministry.

Also from Matthias Media

God is Enough
Refocusing your life

Ray Galea

"What are your disappointments in life? Perhaps, like me, you have unmet superficial desires—perhaps it is achieving that certain position in the company, or getting that high mark in a significant exam. Or maybe you are scarred by grief so profound that you can hardly talk about it. Or perhaps you're not so much disappointed as unmotivated; you have allowed the good and the not so good to hijack the best, and the passionate days of your early Christian life seem so long ago. Whatever the case may be, the issue is the same for all of us: is God enough?"

With honesty and humility, Ray Galea reflects on ten psalms that have helped him put God back in the centre of his life. Ray reminds us of the many reasons we have to join with the psalmist in saying, "Whom have I in heaven but you? And there is nothing on earth that I desire besides you."

For more information or to order contact:

Matthias Media
Email: sales@matthiasmedia.com.au
www.matthiasmedia.com.au

Matthias Media (USA)
Email: sales@matthiasmedia.com
www.matthiasmedia.com

Also from Matthias Media

Nothing in My Hand I Bring
Understanding the differences between Roman Catholic and Protestant beliefs

Ray Galea

When Ray Galea submitted his life to Christ, he had a problem on his hands: Which church should he go to?

> "I did not want to assume that just because I was born a Catholic, this was by definition the right choice. I knew I could just as easily have been born a Baptist or a Mormon. So I spent the next six months reading and talking to priests and ministers to find out the differences between Catholics and Protestants. How did each of their teachings compare with the teaching of Jesus and the apostles?"

This book is a kind of re-tracing of Ray's investigation, looking at the key issues that continue to divide Protestants and Catholics, and assessing them in light of the teaching of Scripture. It is a challenging and invaluable book for Protestants and Catholics alike.

For more information or to order contact:

Matthias Media
Email: sales@matthiasmedia.com.au
www.matthiasmedia.com.au

Matthias Media (USA)
Email: sales@matthiasmedia.com
www.matthiasmedia.com

Also from Matthias Media

The Everlasting Purpose
Broughton Knox

In just under 50 pages, former Principal of Moore Theological College Broughton Knox provides an extraordinarily clear and encouraging explanation of the Bible's teaching on predestination. He shows the comfort, assurance and blessing that flow from understanding the nature of God, the nature of man, and the means of our salvation in Christ.

Broughton Knox's clear thinking and steadfast commitment to the Scriptures will help you make sense of a topic that just about every Christian struggles to understand—let alone explain to others.

First published as 'God who is rich in mercy', a chapter in Broughton Knox's book *The Everlasting God*.

For more information or to order contact:

Matthias Media
Email: sales@matthiasmedia.com.au
www.matthiasmedia.com.au

Matthias Media (USA)
Email: sales@matthiasmedia.com
www.matthiasmedia.com

Also from Matthias Media

Bible studies on Romans

Interactive Bible Studies

Interactive Bible Studies are a bit like a guided tour of a famous city. They take you through a particular part of the Bible, helping you to know where to start, pointing out things along the way, suggesting avenues for further exploration, and making sure that you know how to get home. Like any good tour, the real purpose is to allow you to go exploring for yourself—to dive in, have a good look around, and discover for yourself the riches that God's word has in store.

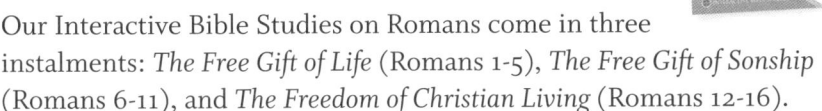

Our Interactive Bible Studies on Romans come in three instalments: *The Free Gift of Life* (Romans 1-5), *The Free Gift of Sonship* (Romans 6-11), and *The Freedom of Christian Living* (Romans 12-16).

Pathway Bible Guides

Pathway Bible Guides are simple, straightforward, easy-to-read Bible studies, ideal for groups who are new to studying the Bible, or groups with limited time for study. We've designed the studies to be short and easy to use, with an uncomplicated vocabulary. At the same time, we've tried to do justice to the passages being studied, and to model good Bible-reading principles.

Peace with God takes us through the key passages in Romans in nine studies, and shows us the great saving power of the God in whom we trust.

FOR MORE INFORMATION OR TO ORDER CONTACT:

Matthias Media
Email: sales@matthiasmedia.com.au
www.matthiasmedia.com.au

Matthias Media (USA)
Email: sales@matthiasmedia.com
www.matthiasmedia.com

Also from Matthias Media

Healed at Last
Separating biblical truth from myth
Scott Blackwell

Meningitis at the age of three left Scott Blackwell with a legacy of serious lifelong health problems, including the severe limp he still walks with. But his physical ailments were only the half of it. By his own admission, he found himself at the age of 18 "tired, starving, sick, experimenting widely with any drug I could find, mildly suicidal and alone".

This book tells how God brought profound healing into Scott Blackwell's life. But it is also the story of Scott's search for what the Bible teaches about physical healing, in this life and the next. Many Christian pastors make strong claims today about God's promise to heal all our physical illnesses. What are we to make of these claims? What does the Bible actually teach about healing?

Scott's examination of these important issues is personal, warm, practical and often funny. But it is also clear, thorough and compelling in its presentation of the Bible's teaching about healing.

Healed at Last offers truth, hope and encouragement for everyone who longs to be healed.

FOR MORE INFORMATION OR TO ORDER CONTACT:

Matthias Media
Email: sales@matthiasmedia.com.au
www.matthiasmedia.com.au

Matthias Media (USA)
Email: sales@matthiasmedia.com
www.matthiasmedia.com